Mr. President

Best wishes,

Ry Bo

Mr. President

A LIFE *of* BENJAMIN HARRISON

RAY E. BOOMHOWER

INDIANA HISTORICAL SOCIETY PRESS | INDIANAPOLIS 2018

© 2018 Indiana Historical Society Press

This book is a publication of the
Indiana Historical Society Press
Eugene and Marilyn Glick Indiana History Center
450 West Ohio Street
Indianapolis, Indiana 45202-3269 USA
www.indianahistory.org
Telephone orders 1-800-447-1830
Fax orders 1-317-234-0562
Online orders @ http://shop.indianahistory.org

Library of Congress Cataloging-in-Publication Data

Names: Boomhower, Ray E., 1959- author.
Title: Mr. President : a life of Benjamin Harrison / Ray E. Boomhower.
Description: Indianapolis : Indiana Historical Society Press, 2018. | Audience: 12-18. | Summary: "In the
    1850s, a young man from Ohio, ready to begin his career as a lawyer, pondered where to practice his new
    profession, considering Cincinnati, Chicago, and Indianapolis. The attorney, Benjamin Harrison, visited
    Indianapolis in March 1854 and decided to make it his home. The choice pleased his father, who wrote his
    son that he would not require any letters of introduction to pave his way, as "the fact is your name is intro-
    duction enough to any of the old inhabitants of Hoosierdom—the old men of Indiana who have become
    patriots of your grandfather and loved him as they loved no other public man." Harrison, who would go on
    in 1888 to win election against incumbent Grover Cleveland, becoming America's twenty-third president,
    seemed destined from birth for national political success. After all, his father had been a two-term congress-
    man from Ohio; his grandfather, William Henry Harrison, served as governor of the Indiana Territory and
    became the country's ninth president; and his great-grandfather, Benjamin Harrison V, had been governor
    of Virginia and one of the signers of the Declaration of Independence"— Provided by publisher. | Includes
    bibliographical references and index.
Identifiers: LCCN 2018004412 (print) | LCCN 2018032106 (ebook) | ISBN 9780871954282 (epub) |
    ISBN 9780871954275 | ISBN 9780871954275q(cloth :qalk. paper)
Subjects: LCSH: Harrison, Benjamin, 1833-1901—Juvenile literature. | Presidents—United States—
    Biography—Juvenile literature.
Classification: LCC E702 (ebook) | LCC E702 .B68 2018 (print) | DDC 973.8/6—dc23
LC record available at https://lccn.loc.gov/2018004412

The paper in this publication meets the minimum requirements of American National Standard for
Information Sciences—Permanence of Paper for Printed Library Materials, ANSI Z39. 48–1984 ∞

As always, for my inspiration in everything, Megan.

Contents

Preface

On a fall day in 1888 the sound of marching feet echoed through the streets of Indianapolis. Armed with red, white, and blue parasols and led by drummers from eleven states, a crowd of approximately 40,000 traveling salesmen marched up North Delaware Street to call upon a local lawyer—a man who had been selected as the Republican Party's nominee for president. As Benjamin Harrison and his wife, Caroline, appeared at the front door of their sixteen-room Italianate-Victorian mansion, the travelers responded with "cheers upon cheers," one eyewitness, Mary Lord Dimmick, remembered later. The cheering lasted until the attorney spoke, Dimmick said, and "then . . . you could have heard a pin drop."

Harrison, who captured the presidency in 1888, defeating incumbent Grover Cleveland, lived in the perfect state to pursue political office, as Indiana played a critical role in national politics during the late-nineteenth and early-twentieth century. Humorist George Ade, paraphrasing a famous statement by Union general William Tecumseh Sherman, noted that the first words of a Hoosier child were: "If nominated I will run, if elected I will serve." As the only president from Indiana, Harrison is well worth becoming part of the Indiana Historical Society Press's Youth Biography Series, targeting readers in middle school and high school.

Since the series began in 2005, it has examined the lives of a wide swath of Hoosier notables, including World War II correspondent Ernie Pyle, religious leader and saint Mother Theodora Guérin, and teacher and lawman Oatess Archey. Other books in the series detailed the life and work of such diverse people as nature writer Gene Stratton-Porter, artist T. C. Steele, AIDS pioneer Ryan White, and beloved basketball coach John Wooden.

The series came about in an unexpected way. In 2003 the IHS, with the support of a grant from the Lilly Endowment Inc., was able to purchase for its William Henry Smith Memorial Library an extensive collection of images and documents of President Abraham Lincoln, including material on the sixteenth president's assassination and the hunt for the conspirators responsible for his death. In addition, the IHS Press worked with the library staff to prepare and issue a coffee-table publication on the collection, titled *Abraham Lincoln Portrayed in the Collections of the Indiana Historical Society*. Taking advantage of some unexpended funds from the Lilly grant, the Press was also able to supplement the Lincoln volume with a book that became the first in the Youth Biography Series, a look at the life of Hoosier politician, general, and writer Lew Wallace. Wallace seemed the perfect choice as a subject, as he had some connection with Lincoln early on in his law career, had served as a major general for the Union cause during the Civil War, and had been a member of the military court that tried the conspirators behind Lincoln's assassination.

In this first book in the series the Press set the stage for the volumes to come in terms of its style of writing and design. In examining other examples of biographies for our target audience, I, as editor of the series, was impressed by the work of the late Newberry Award–winning author Russell Freedman, especially his book *Lincoln: A Photobiography*. Freedman's work featured a clear, concise, and engaging style of writing that I attempted to have each author in the series follow. If any author happened to stumble and call for help, I would advise him or her to imagine trying to make a subject understandable for the average newspaper reader, and tell them to remember William Strunk's most helpful rule: "Omit needless words!" Freedman's book also included another feature we try to highlight in our series—a heavy use of illustrations. The Press is fortunate to be able to draw upon the vast photographic collection of our library, as well as its many maps, postcards, and drawings from the days of the Old Northwest to contemporary times.

I have been lucky enough to write a number of books in the series and have discovered I relish writing for a younger audience (although we have discovered that the biographies appeal to a wide range of readers, especially older adults looking for a concise, but comprehensive, examination of a subject's life and times). What is challenging is providing the proper historical context for younger readers, getting them to realize, as President Harry S Truman once observed, "the only thing new in the world is the history you don't know." Sometimes this involves beginning the tale not with the birth, but with the final few moments of your subject's life, as I did with Pyle and his death from Japanese gunfire during the battle of Okinawa. The worldwide sorrow and grief expressed by soldiers showed just how much respect and admiration the average GI had for the reporter from Indiana.

There always remains, however, the difficulty of connecting today's generation with the past, as the issues seem too wide in scope to be relevant to their lives. One way to establish ties between a reader and a subject is to show that worldwide events affect young individuals in dramatic ways. It is a technique I used in my youth biography about Alex Vraciu of East Chicago, Indiana, who served as a navy fighter pilot in the Pacific. To draw the reader into the story I began the book with the recollection of a young girl who witnessed the Japanese attack on the American fleet at Pearl Harbor, plunging the United States into World War II. I ended the book by telling how a Japanese teenager living in Hiroshima had begun what he thought was a normal morning only to have to deal with the awful destruction unleashed on his city by the dropping by an American B-29 bomber of the first atomic weapon—a development that helped to finally end the war.

Every author who has written a book for the series has drawn upon the skills and talents of a host of people to produce a finished product. This has also been the case for this volume on Harrison. This book would not have been possible without the assistance of the staff at the Benjamin Harrison Presidential Site in Indianapolis, particularly its CEO and president Charles A. Hyde, and its vice president of curatorship and exhibition Jennifer Capps. Indiana author Andrea Neal, who serves on the Harrison site's board of directors, was critical in encouraging me to write the Harrison youth biography. At the IHS Press, able editorial guidance was provided by Kathy Breen and the book's graceful design came from the talents of Isabelle Kroeker and Stacy Simmer. As always, my wife, Megan McKee, has offered wise counsel and invaluable editing, serving as the reader over this author's shoulder.

Timeline of Benjamin Harrison's Life | 1833–1901

August 20, 1833	Born in North Bend, Ohio, to John Scott and Elizabeth Irwin Harrison.
November 3, 1840	William Henry Harrison, Benjamin's grandfather, elected as ninth president of the United States.
March 4, 1841	William Henry inaugurated as president; dies on April 4.
November 3, 1847	Benjamin Harrison attends Farmers' College (previously known as Cary's Academy), located in Cincinnati, Ohio.
August 15, 1850	Elizabeth Harrison dies.
September 30, 1850	Benjamin Harrison enters Miami University, Oxford, Ohio, as a junior. Meets future wife, Caroline (Carrie) Scott.
June 24, 1852	Harrison graduates with honors from Miami University. That fall he reads law with the firm Storer and Gwynne in Cincinnati, Ohio.
October 20, 1853	Harrison marries Caroline Scott.
April 4, 1854	Harrison admitted to the Ohio bar. Moves to Indianapolis to begin his law practice.
August 12, 1854	A son, Russell Harrison, is born.
March 1855	Harrison forms law partnership with William Wallace, brother of Lew Wallace, later author of the best-selling novel *Ben-Hur: A Tale of the Christ*. Harrison appointed commissioner of the Court of the Claims.

May 5, 1857	Elected as city attorney of Indianapolis as a member of the Republican Party.
April 3, 1858	Daughter, Mary (Mamie) Harrison, born.
February 22, 1860	Wins Republican nomination as Supreme Court Reporter for Indiana.
October 9, 1860	Wins election to Supreme Court Reporter position by approximately 9,000 votes.
June 1860	A third child, another daughter, dies at birth.
December 11, 1861	Establishes new law partnership with William P. Fishback.
July 9, 1862	Volunteers for service in Union army during Civil War; appointed second lieutenant to organize Seventieth Indiana Volunteer Infantry Regiment. Promoted to captain on July 22 and colonel on August 8.
Fall 1862	Battles with Confederates at Russellville, Kentucky, and ordered to guard railroad line between Gallatin and Nashville, Tennessee. Prepares men for Union army campaign to take Atlanta, Georgia.
January 2, 1864	Ordered to front with General Joseph Hooker.
February 23, 1864	Renominated for Supreme Court Reporter post.
May 14–15, 1864	Cited for his conduct at the Battle of Resaca. Goes on to win renown for engagements at New Hope Church, Golgotha Church, and Peach Tree Creek.
September 2, 1864	Atlanta captured by Union forces.
September 20, 1864	In Indiana on furlough and confers with Indiana governor Oliver P. Morton. Also campaigns in state for October election.

October 11, 1864	Wins re-election as Supreme Court Reporter.
February 23, 1865	Brevetted as brigadier general.
May 24, 1865	Participates in Grand Review of Union army, Washington, D.C.
June 8, 1865	Receives discharge from army.
July 1865	Joins new law firm of Porter, Harrison, and Fishback, and resumes duties as Supreme Court Reporter.
January 15, 1869	Ends duties as Supreme Court Reporter.
February–March 1869	Serves as prosecutor in Nancy Clem murder case.
May 1871	President Ulysses S. Grant names Harrison to defend U.S. government in Lambdin P. Milligan case.
February–November 1872	Loses nomination for Indiana governor. Campaigns for Grant's re-election.
Fall–Winter 1874	Starts building new home for family on North Delaware Street in Indianapolis.
August 2, 1876	Takes over as Republican candidate for Indiana governor in race against Democrat James D. "Blue Jeans" Williams.
October 10, 1876	Loses governor's race to Williams by approximately 5,000 votes.
July 23–25, 1877	Heads Committee of Public Safety in Indianapolis during railroad strike.
May 26, 1878	Harrison's father, John Scott, dies.
June 28, 1879	President Rutherford B. Hayes appoints Harrison to Mississippi River Commission.

January 17, 1881	Nominated by Indiana legislature as U.S. Senator.
March 4, 1881	Sworn in as U.S. Senator in Washington, D.C.
February 1887	Indiana legislature, now controlled by Democrats, nominates David Turpie to succeed Harrison as senator.
Early 1888	Receives national attention as possible Republican presidential candidate.
June 25, 1888	Wins GOP presidential nomination on eighth ballot at Republican National Convention in Chicago, Illinois. Levi P. Morton of New York selected as Harrison's vice president. Takes on incumbent President Grover Cleveland in fall campaign.
July–October 1888	Delivers numerous campaign speeches to approximately 300,000 visitors to Indianapolis.
October 31, 1888	Infamous "Blocks of Five" scandal hits campaign.
November 6, 1888	Although Harrison loses popular vote to Democrat Cleveland, the Hoosier candidate wins the Electoral College 233 to 168.
February 25, 1889	Departs Indianapolis for inauguration in Washington, D.C.
March 4, 1889	Inaugurated as the twenty-third president. Administered the oath of office by Chief Justice Melville W. Fuller.
	Harrison's cabinet includes Attorney General William H. H. Miller, Postmaster General John Wanamaker, Secretary of the Treasury William Windom, Secretary of State James G. Blaine, Secretary of War Redfield Proctor, Secretary of Navy Benjamin Tracy, Secretary of Agriculture Jeremiah Rusk, and Interior Secretary John W. Noble.

April 29–May 1, 1889	Helps commemorate centennial of President George Washington's first inauguration.
August 22, 1889	Helps dedicate Soldiers and Sailors Monument in Indianapolis.
October 2, 1889	Pan-American Conference begins; adjourned on April 19, 1890.
November 2, 1889	North and South Dakota admitted as thirty-ninth and fortieth states.
November 8, 1889	Montana admitted as forty-first state.
November 11, 1889	Washington becomes forty-second state.
December 3, 1889	In first message to Congress recommends civil-service reform, increased veterans' pensions, civil-rights legislation, and improvements to U.S. Navy.
July 2, 1890	Sherman Anti-Trust Act enacted.
July 3, 1890	Idaho admitted as forty-third state.
July 10, 1890	Wyoming admitted as forty-fourth state.
July 14, 1890	Harrison signs Sherman Silver Purchase Act into law.
July–August 1890	White House undergoes renovation.
October 1, 1890	Congress adjourns; becomes known as "The Billion Dollar Congress" for passing a record number of legislation, including McKinley Tariff.
November 7, 1890	Democrats take over House in off-year election; Republican majority in Senate reduced.
April 14–May 21, 1891	Harrison speaking tour to South and Pacific Northwest covering approximately 9,000 miles; president makes 140 speeches on trip.

October 16, 1891	Incident in Chile involves sailors on shore leave from USS *Baltimore*, causing tense relations between the two countries.
January 26, 1892	Chile situation resolved.
May 23, 1892	Decides to seek renomination from GOP for another term as president. Secretary of State Blaine resigns on June 4, three days before start of Republican National Convention in Minneapolis, Minnesota.
June 7–10, 1892	Harrison renominated for president on first ballot. Whitelaw Reid of New York nominated as vice president.
June 22, 1892	Democratic National Convention in Chicago nominates Cleveland as presidential candidate with Adlai E. Stevenson of Illinois as vice president.
July 6, 1892	Violence breaks out at Homestead Works of the Carnegie Steel Company near Pittsburgh. On July 12, more violence occurs during strike at silver mines at Coeur d'Alene, Idaho.
Summer 1892	Caroline Harrison gravely ill with tuberculosis.
October 25, 1892	Caroline Harrison dies at White House; burial follows in Indianapolis at Crown Hill Cemetery.
November 8, 1892	Harrison loses presidency to Cleveland in national election. Loses both popular vote and Electoral College.
March 4, 1893	Harrison attends Cleveland's inauguration and returns to Indianapolis.
Spring 1894	Delivers law lectures at Stanford University in California.

June 10, 1895	Harrison appointed as a trustee of Purdue University.
Winter 1895	Announces engagement to Mary Lord Dimmick.
April 27, 1896	Marries Dimmick in ceremonies at Saint Thomas Episcopal Church in New York City.
Summer 1896	Publishes series of articles in *Ladies' Home Journal*.
November 3, 1896	Republican William McKinley elected as twenty-fifth president of the United States with his vice president, Theodore Roosevelt.
January 1898	Harrison agrees to represent Venezuela in border dispute with Great Britain. Argues case in Paris, June–September 1899.
March 3–9, 1901	Falls ill with pneumonia.
March 13, 1901	Harrison dies at his home on North Delaware Street, Indianapolis.
March 17, 1901	Burial at Crown Hill Cemetery.

1

"He's All Right"

In the spring of 1873 Thomas R. Marshall, a student at Wabash College in Crawfordsville, Indiana, found himself in deep trouble. Working as an editor for the college's bimonthly newspaper, *The Geyser*, Marshall had written an article making fun of a visiting temperance speaker and teacher of elocution named Ida Leggett. He had accused the married woman of playing "footsie" (flirting) under a table with students living at a boardinghouse where she was staying.

Writing in a period when journalism, he admitted, was "in its incipient stage," Marshall played to his readers' basic instincts with his article. Featured in the student newspaper's March 19, 1873, issue, his piece claimed that Leggett had "shown her cloven foot at last. Though the cause of her departure was kept a secret for several days, it leaked out at last. She was caught tramping on the feet of the boys boarding at her house and was immediately kicked out. We have nothing to say, however, as she gave us the worth of our money in her entertainments."

Outraged by what she had read, Leggett hired a respected local lawyer, Lew Wallace, a Civil War general and future best-selling author and diplomat, to bring a lawsuit against Marshall and the rest of the *Geyser* staff for libel. She sought $20,000 in damages. Realizing the trouble he was in, Marshall, upon the urging of his fellow codefendants, sought legal aid. He traveled to Indianapolis to ask for advice from an attorney praised as having "no superior at the bar of Indiana." That lawyer was Benjamin Harrison.

Like Wallace, Harrison had risen to the rank of general in the Union army and had also earned a reputation as a fine public speaker on behalf of the Republican Party after the war. "Some speakers had more fire, and some more magnetism, but few were more graceful and convincing in their motive," said Reverend Ferdinand Cowle Iglehart in a magazine article on Harrison. GOP (Grand Old Party) leaders held great expectations for Harrison's future in politics. Marshall met with Harrison, showed him the article, and asked his opinion about whether or not it might be libelous. Remembering the meeting years later in his autobiography, Marshall said that Harrison carefully read the piece, looked up at him, and said: "Young man, if I had an enemy that I wanted to libel and could hire you to look after the job, I would not hunt further."

A shaky Marshall explained to Harrison that he had no hope of raising 20,000 cents, let alone 20,000 dollars, if he lost the case. "He said I would have to justify the article by proof of the truth of what was written or have a big judgment which some time I would have to pay or have it everlastingly hanging over my head," Marshall recalled. Luckily for the Wabash student, Harrison agreed to represent the young journalists. When the case was heard in New York, and after initial testimony had been given, Leggett withdrew her lawsuit.

A relieved Marshall, who later rose to prominence in the Democratic Party, serving as Indiana governor and for two terms as vice president under Woodrow Wilson, asked Harrison what he owed him for his services. He added that he could write his father to secure the needed funds. "Not a cent," Harrison responded. "I wouldn't think of taking anything from you. You have been foolish boys and this will be a great lesson to you. Never hereafter in life charge anybody with wrongdoing or crime that you do not have in your hands undoubted proof that it is true before you make the charge, and even then don't make it unless you are quite satisfied that by the making of it you are either defending yourself or performing some real public service."

Marshall had learned a valuable lesson. He had also developed a lifelong respect for Harrison, who fifteen years later captured the nation's highest office, winning the 1888 election as America's twenty-third chief executive and becoming its centennial president—inaugurated a hundred years after George Washington.

As Benjamin once told a friend, the "prevailing over-ruling characteristic" of his young life had been "a determination to succeed in spite of every human obstacle. . . . A faint heart never did anything worthy

Benjamin Harrison, 1888, the year he was elected as the nation's twenty-third president in spite of being outvoted in his home city of Indianapolis by Democrat challenger Grover Cleveland.

of a man." He vowed to himself to never "falter in my purpose. I have long since made up my mind that with God's blessing and good health, I would succeed, and I never allow myself to doubt the results."

Given Hoosiers' love of politics, and the famous Harrison name, it was perhaps inevitable that the young Harrison became drawn—reluctantly at first— into running for public office. In 1856 some Republican friends arrived at Harrison's law office and dragged the attorney away from his work to speak before a political gathering. Introduced to the crowd as the grandson of "Old Tippecanoe," Harrison firmly replied: "I want it understood that I am the grandson of nobody. I believe that every man should stand on his own merits." To him achieving fame and fortune would only be truly honorable and desirable if it were earned.

Later, when a close acquaintance asked him if he had ever seriously thought of being president, Harrison responded that the "thought had been with him many times when suggested by others, but he had never been possessed by it or had his life shaped by it."

LIBRARY OF CONGRESS

Lithograph of Harrison's service during the Civil War at the Battle of Resaca, created by the Chicago firm of Kurz and Allison, circa 1880s.

The Harrison family's strong political background, however, did aid Harrison when he undertook a career in politics, becoming Indianapolis city attorney in 1857 and elected to the post of Indiana Supreme Court Reporter three years later. In July 1862, a year after the outbreak of the American Civil War, Indiana governor Oliver P. Morton asked Harrison to recruit men for the Seventieth Indiana Volunteer Infantry Regiment. "I love to feel [I am] in some humble way serving a country which has brought so many honors to my kindred and such untold blessings to those I love," said Harrison.

He eventually served as the regiment's colonel, receiving the nickname "Little Ben" from his troops (he stood approximately five feet, six inches tall), and offered sterling service at the battles of Peach Tree Creek and Resaca, Georgia. He wrote his wife, Caroline "Carrie" Scott Harrison, whom he had married in 1853, that he was prepared to give his life to the cause. If that happened, he told her to let her grief be lessened "by the consolation that I died for my country and in Christ. If God gives me strength I mean to bear myself bravely, and come what will, so that you may have no cause to blush for me, though you should be forced to mourn."

During his service, Harrison earned a name for tough discipline tempered by deep concern for his men's well-being, a reputation that followed him to the presidency. One of his biographers noted that as an officer Harrison was "a stern, yet fair, taskmaster who knew that idleness was waste and that civilians do not become soldiers simply by putting on uniforms." A captain serving in the Seventieth remembered on long, tiring marches seeing his commanding officer, Harrison, carrying the equipment of "some poor worn out solider," as well as dismounting and walking "while a sick soldier occupied his place on the horse." His service in the war was an important part of the rest of his life, with Harrison often speaking at meetings of the Grand Army of the Republic, the fraternal organization for Union army veterans. "I know of no higher honor in the world," Harrison said, "than to be called 'comrade' by the survivors of those who saved the Union."

After mustering out of the Union army, Harrison returned to Indianapolis, reestablished his lucrative law practice, and became a force in Republican politics in the state. He was often called upon to give speeches on behalf of the party. A friend recalled that he would always remember how Harrison appeared when pleading for a cause in which he was deeply engaged: "The face, pale and tense; the eyes, blue and piercing; the voice, incisive and penetrating, and the words charged with thought and feeling and conviction, until at last he made an appeal which moved men to action." Although he lost a race for Indiana governor in 1876, just a few years later the state legislature, controlled by the GOP, picked Harrison to serve a six-year term in the U.S. Senate.

Harrison arrived on the national political scene at a favorable time, as the nineteenth state played a key role during the late nineteenth and early twentieth centuries in helping decide presidential contests, with both parties selecting Hoosiers to bolster their chances in November. From 1840 to 1940 almost 60 percent of the national elections had Indiana politicians on the ballot. Also, as an "October state" from 1851 through 1880, with elections for state and local officials held a month before the regular election, Indiana offered political parties a sounding board on the mood of

Harrison speaking near the train depot in Bloomington, Indiana, 1896.

Harrison supporters display an umbrella emblazoned with lyrics from the Republican candidate's campaign song.

voters. Party loyalty was expected of every man eligible to vote (women could not exercise their franchise until the 1920s). "Unless free government is discreditable," said Harrison, "it is the duty of every American citizen to support that party to which he gives the allegiance of his heart and mind."

In June 1888, at the Republican National Convention in Chicago, delegates, after seven ballots, selected Harrison as their party's presidential candidate against incumbent Democrat Grover Cleveland. James G. Blaine, who had been the party's presidential candidate in 1884, had ruled out another run for the White House, leaving the nomination open for Harrison. "The one man remaining who in my judgment can make the best run is Benjamin Harrison," Blaine said before the convention. Writing about Harrison's nomination, however, a Republican newspaper was low key about the candidate, noting, "Some men are born great, some achieve greatness, some have greatness thrust upon them, and others live in pivotal states." GOP supporters were soon singing in praise of their candidate, "Oh, what's the matter with Harrison? / He's all right / There can be no comparison / He's all right."

Possessed with a strong Christian faith, Harrison became known for honest dealings during a time when corruption in politics was commonplace. Writing his son, Russell, after he had suffered some financial setbacks, Harrison advised him not to let financial pressures undermine his sense of honor, duty, and faith in God. "It is a great comfort to trust God—even if His providence is unfavorable," Harrison wrote. "Prayer steadies one when he is walking in slippery places—even if things asked for are not given."

Although admired for his faith and honesty, Harrison sometimes was viewed by even his supporters as reserved and aloof, while his opponents referred to him as a "human iceberg." A close associate, William H. H. Miller, who served as attorney general in his administration, said Harrison was not "a *cordial* man" with anybody except his close friends. Often, even when dispensing favors, Harrison caused ill feelings with his brusque behavior, and seemed to possess a talent for "doing the right thing in the wrong way." On one occasion, a person close to the president warned a visitor before meeting with Harrison, "Don't feel insulted by anything he may do or say . . . it is only his way." A historian of his administration described Harrison's manner perfectly when he noted that he "preferred directness, simplicity, and unusual frankness; and he unnecessarily made enemies in the process." One of his Republican friends noted that if Harrison spoke to a crowd of 10,000 his oratorical skills could make everyone in the audience his friend, but "if he were introduced to each of them afterward each would depart his enemy." Another Republican, Chauncey Depew, said Harrison's stiff personal manner was due to the fact that his career had been "one of battle, from his early struggles to his triumphant success."

In his dealings with the press, Harrison could also seem remote. Hilton U. Brown, who covered Harrison for the *Indianapolis News*, recalled that the general "never toadied nor flattered and could be flatfooted and hardheaded to the press when he thought best to decline to be interviewed, or to venture random or casual remarks." Brown added that when agreeing to give remarks "off the record," Harrison's manner changed dramatically, and he could be "as gracious as any man in public life of that period." Also,

459-465 Penn Ave.
Washington, D.C.

Before serving as Harrison's attorney general, William H. H. Miller studied law with Chief Justice of the Supreme Court Morrison Waite and practiced law for a time in Peru, Indiana.

the newspaperman observed, Harrison, when dealing with former comrades in arms, fellow church members, and those he knew from his college days, "revealed a genuine warmth of sentiment not suspected by some of his contemporaries. Life to him was full of purpose and he could not be deflected from an objective: but there were 'hours of ease' when he paid homage to his friends and to friendship."

Harrison knew he could be seen as unsympathetic but refused to change his personality for image's sake. Several years before he became president, he was on his way to give a political speech in an Indiana city. Before leaving Indianapolis, his friend, John C. New, one of the few people who called him by his first name, advised him: "Now Ben. I know you'll capture them with your speech, but for God's sake be a human being down there. Mix around a little with the boys after the meeting." A few days after his return, Harrison saw New and said to him: "John, I tried it, but I failed. I'll never try again. I must be myself."

Known for his humor during his time as vice president under President Woodrow Wilson, Thomas R. Marshall once joked: "Once there were two brothers. One ran away to sea; the other was elected vice president of the United States. And nothing was heard of either of them again."

Marshall, known for having a well-developed wit, believed that the reports of Harrison having a "cold-blooded nature" were unfounded. Often, Harrison was "too busy thinking, reasoning, seeking the right, to be a light-hearted man such as I am," Marshall recalled. Whatever anyone might have thought of him, Marshall believed that Harrison's "heart beat true to all the finer and nobler instincts of our nature." The owner of a boardinghouse where Harrison had stayed in Washington, D.C., while serving in the U.S. Senate, admired his independence. He noted that at dinner other senators (whom he did not name) passed Harrison by without speaking "as though they didn't care a d–n for him. But what I liked about Harrison was, that he didn't seem to care a G–d d––n for them."

When those he knew well were in trouble, Harrison was quick to offer his support. When his private secretary as president, Elijah Halford, became ill, Harrison invited him and his wife to stay in the White House until he had recovered. When the president heard that the home of Secretary of the Navy Benjamin Tracy had caught fire, he rushed to the scene and performed artificial respiration on Tracy, saving his life. The fire killed Tracy's wife and daughter, and the president invited the distraught

Tracy to recover at the White House. "Few men had quicker, warmer, or more delicate sympathies," said Halford.

In spite of his icy reputation, Harrison attracted enthusiastic support from his fellow Hoosiers during the 1888 campaign. Just moments after learning of Harrison's nomination, a "surging throng of excited and yelling men" packed the streets of Indianapolis, eventually making their way to his downtown law office, with many surging inside to shake the candidate's hand. Like most presidential contenders of that time, Harrison declined to barnstorm around the country for votes, preferring to remain at his home on North Delaware Street on the city's north side. "I have a great risk of

A crowd, including a delegation from Danville, Indiana, gathers at Harrison's home on North Delaware Street in Indianapolis a few hours after he had received the Republican nomination for president, June 25, 1888. Harrison is standing near the front door slightly to the left.

"Protection for American Labor" campaign ribbon touting Republican candidates Harrison and Levi P. Morton in the 1888 election.

meeting a fool at home," he told journalist Whitelaw Reid," but the candidate who travels cannot escape him."

That fall Harrison, from his front stoop and at a nearby public park, gave more than ninety speeches to approximately 300,000 visitors—"spontaneous pilgrimages," as the candidate called them—who flocked to see him. By the end of the campaign Harrison confessed to his running mate, Levi P. Morton, a wealthy banker from New York, that he had grown "quite tired of hearing my own voice." He joked that even at home when he sat down to eat with his family he had "some apprehensions lest someone may propose a toast and insist that I respond."

Although Harrison received approximately 90,000 fewer popular votes than Cleveland, the Hoosier candidate carried the Electoral College, receiving 233 votes to 168 for his opponent. Harrison narrowly captured his home state, winning by 2,348 votes out of 536,964 cast. As a key state for both parties in the election, Indiana, noted one historian, had been reduced to a "pitiable condition of political corruption . . . and both the great parties had been exhausting the resources of political depravity to carry it." This included relying on people known as "floaters," voters with no fixed party loyalty who sold their vote to the highest bidder. Corruption had become so commonplace in the Hoosier State that those working at the grassroots level for the party of choice sometimes offered as proof of their loyalty the fact that they had risked going to jail on its behalf.

After the close election, in which 79.3 percent of the population eligible to vote went to the polls, Harrison seemed blissfully unaware that political shenanigans might have played a role in his rise to the presidency. He told U.S. Senator Matt Quay of Pennsylvania, GOP national chairman, that "Providence has given us victory." Quay, a veteran politician who considered the new president a "political tenderfoot," was not moved by Harrison's oratory. He later exclaimed to a Philadelphia journalist, "Think of the man! He ought to know that Providence hadn't a damn thing to do with it." Harrison, Quay said, "would never know how close a number of men were compelled to approach the gates of the penitentiary to make him President." In spite of the charges of corruption swirling around the campaign, none of the stink clung to Harrison. A New York Republican Party official predicted great things for Harrison's presidency, noting, "Every wage earner pleads more freely, every soldier of the Union holds his head a little higher and I believe Republicans everywhere

Described as a "kingmaker" by Harrison, Pennsylvania political boss Matt Quay twice served in the U.S. Senate, from 1887 to 1899 and 1901 to his death in 1904.

stand ready to help in upholding your hands in the great work to which
Providence has called you."

Harrison firmly believed that the policies of the Republican Party
possessed the best means to improve life for the nation's citizens and
worked to promote them as an activist, hands-on chief executive for both
domestic matters and foreign affairs. "I do not know how our institutions
could endure," he said, "unless we so conduct our public affairs and society
that every man who is sober and industrious shall be able to make a good,
comfortable living and lay something aside for old age and evil days; to
have hope in their heart and better prospects for his children. . . . Whatever
promotes that I want to favor." Harrison took on additional responsibilities
in foreign affairs due to the often poor health of Secretary of State Blaine.
As an Indianapolis newspaper noted, the president possessed "higher views
of the functions of administration than the beaten path of routine and
precedent." Harrison's administration had some impressive achievements,
including passage of the Sherman Antitrust Act to limit business
monopolies, the admission of six western states into the Union in 1889
and 1890, the establishment of thirteen million acres as forest reserves and
national parks, modernizing the American navy, and negotiating several
trade agreements with other countries.

During his administration Harrison also sought to improve voting
rights for African Americans—an act one historian called "the most
courageous stand by any president of his era in favor of black Americans."
In his message to Congress in December 1889, Harrison asked: "When and
under what conditions is the black man to have a free ballot? When is he in
fact to have those full civil rights which had so long been his in law? When
is that equality of influence which our form of government was intended
to secure to the electors to be restored?" Harrison backed up these strong
words with action, appointing legendary African American social reformer

and ex-slave Frederick Douglass as U.S. minister (today ambassador) to Haiti, as well as William D. McCoy, an Indianapolis black leader, as U.S. minister to Liberia. Unfortunately, legislation authorizing federal oversight of congressional contests to ensure that African American voters would receive equal treatment failed in the Senate, but Harrison's effort in that regard "should endear him to the colored people as long as he lives," said Douglass.

As First Lady, Caroline Scott Harrison also added luster to her husband's administration, fighting to improve a White House that had fallen into disrepair and advocating on behalf of the fine arts. In addition, she worked to secure admission for women into the Johns Hopkins Medical School and served as the first president-general of a fledgling organization—the Daughters of the American Revolution, which had been formed after the Sons of the American Revolution had declined to admit women applicants. Since its formation in 1890, the DAR has worked to secure and preserve "the historical spots of America and the erection thereon of suitable monuments to perpetuate the memories of the heroic deeds of the men and women who aided the revolution and created constitutional government in America."

No less an authority than Henry Adams, the distinguished American historian and diplomat,

BENJAMIN HARRISON PRESIDENTIAL SITE

Portrait of Caroline Scott Harrison taken by Indianapolis photographer W. H. Potter.

considered Harrison to be "an excellent President, a man of ability and force; perhaps the best President the Republican Party had put forward since [Abraham] Lincoln's death." For all of his successes, however, Harrison faced an uphill fight when he sought another four years in office, running for a second term with Cleveland once again as his opponent. Although Republican officials wanted the president to undertake an aggressive campaign, he could not, as his wife was battling an illness— tuberculosis—that eventually led to her death on October 25, 1892. "Politics and business have been crowding me day and night," Harrison wrote his daughter, "and with the anxiety about your mother, makes life just now a burden and ambition a delusion." Harrison had even considered refusing to run for a second term, but, responding to slurs against his leadership, had decided to persevere, telling a political ally, "No Harrison has ever retreated in the presence of a foe without giving battle, and so I have determined to stand and fight."

The Republicans' legislative efforts had been blocked when the party lost in midterm elections in 1890. Labor unrest two years later in the steel industry and at silver mines in the West hurt the incumbent's campaign, as did a last-minute announcement from leading Hoosier Republican (and Harrison rival) Walter Q. Gresham that he had decided to support the Democratic presidential candidate. Harrison lost his rematch with Cleveland, losing both the popular vote and in the Electoral College, 277 to 145; the president even lost his home state, Indiana, as well as such pivotal states as New York, New Jersey, and Connecticut. Cleveland also captured Illinois and Wisconsin, the first post-Civil War Democrat to do so. Harrison seemed almost relieved about his defeat, noting that the result was more "surprising to the victor than to me. For me there is not sting in it. Indeed after the heavy blow the death of my wife dealt me I do not think I could have stood the strain a re-election would have brought."

Harrison received a hero's welcome upon his return to Indianapolis, where he reestablished a flourishing law practice. As an ex-president, Harrison kept busy by preparing lectures on constitutional law for Stanford University, helping to propel the young institution to national prominence; writing articles about voting that appeared in the *Ladies' Home Journal*, one of the country's leading magazines; serving as a trustee for Purdue University; and representing the Republic of Venezuela in a border dispute with Great Britain. In that time, he refused all attempts to get him to run again for public office. "I do not see anything but labor and worry and distress in another campaign or another term in the White House," he said.

BENJAMIN HARRISON PRESIDENTIAL SITE

A fellow Republican politician once said of Harrison that he was the only man who served as president "capable of discharging with signal ability the duty of every one of his cabinet ministers."

At the age of sixty-two in 1896, he found personal happiness in a second marriage—with Mary Scott Dimmick, the widowed niece of his deceased wife, with whom he had a daughter, Elizabeth.

In early 1901 Harrison fell sick with influenza that later worsened into pneumonia. He died on March 13 in his Indianapolis home at the age of sixty-seven. According to his obituary in the *New York Times*, the former president's "death was quiet and painless, there being a gradual sinking until the end came, which was marked by a single gasp for breath as life departed from the body of the great statesman." At Harrison's funeral at Indianapolis's

In 1964 the U.S. Department of the Interior designated Harrison's Indianapolis home, today the Benjamin Harrison Presidential Site, as a National Historic Landmark.

First Presbyterian Church, and before his eventual burial at Crown Hill Cemetery in a grave next to his first wife, Caroline, he was eulogized by another Indiana legend, the Hoosier Poet himself, James Whitcomb Riley. One particular characteristic Harrison possessed impressed Riley—"his fearless independence and stand for what he believed to be right and just. . . . A fearless man inwardly commands respect, and above everything else Harrison was fearless and just."

Today, the achievements of Harrison as president are preserved and promoted by the Benjamin Harrison Presidential Site, which has been open to the public since the 1950s. Unveiled to the public on October 27, 1908, a monument to Harrison on the south edge of University Park stands in remembrance of a man, noted former Vice President Charles W. Fairbanks, who represented what was best in public and private life, someone of "pure purpose, scorning the ignoble and seeking always to lift his fellows to an exalted plane of life and effort." On its base are featured remarks Harrison made in honor of his old supreme commander during the Civil War, General Ulysses S. Grant. The words read: "Great lives do not go out. They go on."

2

"my own cherished home"

On Monday, February 25, 1889, a special Pennsylvania Railroad car, Number 120, decorated with rich furnishings that made it "a veritable Oriental palace," awaited the arrival of a special passenger. That passenger, one of Indianapolis's leading citizens, found himself quite emotional that morning as he prepared to leave his beloved city. Benjamin Harrison, who had first made the city his home as a young lawyer in April 1854, had, just a few months earlier, won the nation's highest office—president. According to his personal secretary, Elijah Halford, Harrison, all alone in his private library for a time, seemed "badly broken up . . . and full of tears when the time came to take his leave" from his comfortable home on North Delaware Street for the journey to the White House.

While Harrison dealt with his emotions, a large, enthusiastic crowd gathered outside to follow him as his carriage traveled the fifteen blocks to Union Station, passing along the way houses decorated with flags and bunting for the occasion. By the time he left his home with his wife, Caroline, and other members of his family, Harrison had regained his composure. "His ever cool and collected manner manifested itself," noted the *Indianapolis Journal*, "and yet not interfering with his appreciation of kind and friendly remarks that often took the form of witty allusions." Other news accounts noted that citizens waved banners, fired guns, and waved their handkerchiefs from downtown windows and balconies at the procession. When the carriage reached the Denison Hotel, members of the Indiana General Assembly saluted Harrison and followed the carriage on foot. Before the train left the station, Harrison, from the railroad car's rear platform, gave a brief talk to those waving goodbye. He said:

> I love this city. It has been my own cherished home. Twice before I have left it to discharge public duties and returned to it with gladness, as I hope to do again. It is a city on whose streets the pompous displays of wealth are not seen. It is full of pleasant homes, and in these homes there is an unusual store of contentment.
>
> The memory of your favor and kindness will abide with me and my strong desire to hold your respect and confidence will strengthen me in the discharge of my new and responsible duties. Let me say farewell to all my Indiana friends. For the public honors that have come to me I am their grateful debtor. They have made the debt so large that I can never discharge it.
>
> There is a great sense of loneliness in the discharge of high public duties. The moment of decision is one of isolation. But there is One whose help comes even into the quiet chamber of judgment, and to His wise and unfailing guidance will I look for direction and safety.

As the train moved away from the station, the *Journal* reported that the crowd followed it as far as it could, waving hats and handkerchiefs. "The last glimpse of the rear platform to be had from the station," said the newspaper, "showed . . . Harrison standing by the rail with Mrs. Harrison by his side, both waving their handkerchiefs in response to similar salutations from the crowds that lined the way." Harrison was on his way to take the oath of office as the twenty-third president of the United States.

* * *

The elevation of Benjamin Harrison, born on August 20, 1833, in North Bend, Ohio, to the presidency seemed to be part of his birthright, as he was a member of an illustrious family in the country's history. By the time young Ben turned seven, his grandfather, William Henry Harrison, the hero of the Battle of Tippecanoe, had taken the oath of office as the ninth president of the United States (he died only a month after taking office). The family tree also included Benjamin Harrison V, who represented Virginia in the Continental Congress and signed the Declaration of Independence. John Scott Harrison, the only person to be the child and the parent of a U.S. president, also tasted political success, serving two terms in Congress from 1853 to 1857.

In addition to becoming president, William Henry Harrison served as governor of the Indiana Territory and as a congressman and U.S. senator from Ohio.

BENJAMIN HARRISON PRESIDENTIAL SITE

Young Ben was the second child and second son born to John Scott and Elizabeth Irwin Harrison, devoted followers of the Presbyterian faith. Until Elizabeth's death in 1850, her children were used to hearing her daily prayer: "May God bless you and keep you continually under His protecting care." Ben spent his childhood on land his father farmed that had been carved out of William Henry's 2,000-acre estate at North Bend, an area known as The Point, located between the Big Miami and Ohio Rivers.

On his farm John Scott, who had been trained as a lawyer, raised corn, wheat, and hay, and kept pigs and cattle. His young son did the usual farm

Benjamin Harrison V, the father of William Henry Harrison and great-grandfather of Benjamin Harrison, served as the fifth governor of Virginia.

chores, including rising early in the morning to feed the livestock and to harvest crops. A congressman who had also spent his boyhood on a southern Ohio farm recalled that Ben, to deliver a sack of wheat to the local mill, balanced the sack "over the horse's back by getting on one end of it, holding on the horse's mane while he was going up hill, and feeling anxious about the results."

John Scott struggled to make a living at times. He wrote to his brother-in-law that his "lot in this life has been to raise hogs and hominy [coarsely ground corn] to feed my children and I have devoted but little time to *fancy articles*." A family friend blamed John Scott's financial troubles on "the consequence of his generosity and a judgment too easily cheated by people who wormed their way into his confidence." John Scott seldom failed, however, to find the funds necessary to educate his children, hiring private tutors and giving them access to his private library, which was liberally stocked with books on American history and biography. He also faithfully offered his son advice throughout his career, even while busy representing his constituents as a U.S. Congressman.

One of the Harrison family's tutors, Harriet Root, remembered Ben as the brightest of the bunch. Even at the age of five years old, she said that he was determined to get ahead in everything. Although Root said he could be "terribly stubborn about many things," insisting on having his own

View of North Bend, Ohio, looking up the Ohio River with the Kentucky hills in the distance.

Benjamin Harrison's boyhood home, the Point Farm.

John Scott and Elizabeth Harrison.

way, she had only one bit of serious trouble from him. She solved that by turning him over to his mother. "She corrected him and he came back quite submissive," Root remembered, "and never gave me any more trouble."

In the fall of 1847 John Scott sent his two oldest sons, Irwin, sixteen, and Ben, fourteen, to further their education at a small secondary school, Farmers' College (previously known as Cary's Academy), located in Cincinnati, Ohio. At the time of his attendance at the school, Ben was described by one biographer as being of "slight physique, slender and not tall," but making up for "these deficiencies, if such they may be called, by spirit, wit, and ready knowledge of character." Ben stayed at the school for three years, falling under the influence of one of its finest teachers, Doctor Robert Hamilton Bishop, who taught history and political economy. "Education," Bishop told his students, "is getting possession of your mind, so you can use facts as the good mechanic uses his tools." He also urged them, when speaking either privately or publically, to make remarks that others would remember—something Ben put to good use in his subsequent political career.

While at Farmers' College, Ben, through Bishop, met another teacher, Doctor John W. Scott, who taught chemistry and physics and had been responsible for organizing a women's college. Ben was soon a frequent visitor in the Scott household, drawn, in no small part, by one of Scott's daughters, Caroline, and her "dancing brown eyes." With lessons from her aunt, Caroline became a talented artist, as well as musician. A romance blossomed between Ben and Caroline, but was interrupted when Scott moved his family to Oxford, Ohio, founding the Oxford Female Institute, where Caroline attended classes.

Shortly after his seventeenth birthday, and dazed with grief at the death of his mother, who had died on August 15, 1850, at the age of forty, Ben traveled to Oxford, Ohio, to begin studies as a junior at Miami University, known as the "Yale of the West" for its distinguished liberal-arts curriculum. The university, which had welcomed its first students in 1824, boasted that it offered courses that were "full and thorough in all departments, and equal in these respects to any college in the United States." It had strict rules for its students, who were forbidden from leaving their rooms from 7:00 p.m. until chapel services at 7:30 a.m. John Scott also offered advice to his son, writing that he should give "diligent attention" to his studies, and, in dealing with his classmates, never "seek

Old main building exterior from the northwest, circa 1896, Miami University, Oxford, Ohio.

to make a witty remark at the expense of the feelings of a less gifted friend or acquaintance." Ben followed his father's counsel, earning a reputation as one of the three brightest students at the university, along with David Swing and Milton Saylor.

Among his classmates, Ben was seen as a level-headed young man who could "see clearly, think well on his feet," as well as possessing "a vocabulary of apt words constantly at his command." Lewis W. Ross, who had attended Farmers' College with Ben and had also gone on to Miami, remembered him as "an unpretentious but courageous student," who "never seemed to regard life as a joke nor the opportunities for advancement as subjects for sport." Although in his political career Harrison was sometimes described as cold-hearted, Ross believed that his fellow classmate's career had represented the principles that governed his student life: "He was just then. He is just now. He was industrious then. He is industrious now. He was ambitious then. He is ambitious still." Harrison's only vice seemed to be his habit of smoking long cigars, something his father viewed with displeasure, as had his mother.

Life in Oxford included a continued romance with Caroline, who was attending the Oxford Female Institute, from which she graduated with degrees in music, art, and literature. Although as head of the institute Doctor Scott had attempted to keep the young men from Miami away from his charges, including locking the gate upon nightfall, his daughter convinced him to allow the two sexes to mingle. Both Ben and Caroline possessed serious natures, but Caroline, perhaps due to her artistic nature, loved to dance. Such an activity, she remembered, "was considered a great sin at Oxford." On one occasion, when the couple had slipped away for a buggy ride while Caroline's parents were away from home, she took Ben to a party. She danced the hours away, while he remained on the sidelines.

Before receiving his degree with honors from Miami on June 24, 1852, the nineteen-year-old Harrison pondered what to do with his life after graduation. He and Caroline had become secretly engaged (they married on October 20, 1853), and he needed to make a living. Harrison considered three possible professions: the ministry, physics, or the law. Although he realized that the "legal profession has not yet arrived at that dignity and moral excellence to which it could be brought," he decided to become an attorney. He made his choice with the belief that he could maintain his strong Christian faith while also being successful in such a profession. "Fellow Christians," he said in a speech to Miami students, "if you adopt this Prof[ession], let me effectively entreat you to remember that you are to do all to the glory of God."

Benjamin Harrison at age twenty-one.

Harrison's choice proved to be a momentous one. The law became the main source of his income for the rest of his life, during and especially after his term as president. (Ex-presidents received no pension for their service until 1958, when the Former Presidents Act provided those who had not been removed from office several lifetime benefits, including a pension.) In addition, becoming a lawyer often helped open doors for those who wanted to enter the world of politics—always a popular pastime in nineteenth-century America. Politics had been on Harrison's mind as a Miami student, and he was determined, as with the law, to be guided by his faith while engaged in the activity. He noted that civil society was no "less an institution of God than the Church, that society can in no sense exist without government, and that man is the instrumentality appointed to administer this government." Although the church itself should take "no part in the affairs of state," he said, its individual members, "as embodying the only true morality and as members of civil society, owe to that society of which they form an integral part certain duties for the neglect of which God will not hold them guiltless."

In the nineteenth century, someone interested in becoming a lawyer often bypassed law school and instead "read law" with a practicing attorney before taking exams and being admitted to the bar. Harrison's father sent his son to Cincinnati to see one of his friends, Bellamy Storer, a former congressman and senior member of the law firm of Storer and Gwynne. Storer agreed to take him on, and Harrison set to work. Responding to a letter from his sister, Anna, who asked how he spent his day, Ben answered:

> I don't think it would interest you very much. I do the same things every day . . . eat three meals . . . sleep six hours and read dusty old books the rest of the time. . . . If you could see me in my office my feet cocked up and a big book with a brown paper cover on it in my lap . . . you would think me a picture of content. I suppose you have read about the Great Desert. Well, my life is about as barren of anything funny as the Great Desert is of grass.

In April 1854 Harrison was formally admitted to the Ohio bar and pondered where to practice his new profession, considering Cincinnati, Chicago, and Indianapolis. At first, he looked to Chicago as the favorite. Harrison wrote for advice to a Chicago attorney, Thomas B. Bryan, who wrote back that to "succeed here in a strange city without friends might prove more difficult or at least require the exercise of great patience than to attain success where the fame of your Grandfather and the excellent character of your Father are so well known and appreciated." With Chicago out of the running, Harrison also decided he could not stay in Cincinnati. "I long to cut my leading strings and acquire an identity of my own," he wrote a friend. "Were I to continue on here, it would be long ere that people should cease to regard me as a boy, and almost as long ere I should cease to regard myself as such."

Harrison visited Indianapolis in March 1854 and decided to make it his and Caroline's home. The choice pleased his father. John Scott wrote his son that he would not require any letters of introduction to pave his way, as "the fact is your *name* is introduction enough to any of the old inhabitants of Hoosierdom—the old men of Indiana who have become patriots of your grandfather and loved him as they loved no other public man." Harrison had also received encouragement from one of his cousins, William Sheets, a successful Indianapolis businessman, who said the city "promises more, in the future, than almost any other place in the West." Sheets added that any young professional man who decided to make Indianapolis his residence "and be content to grow with this place, must, in my judgment, succeed." He also informed Harrison of an important fact—most members of the city's legal profession were "moral, and some of them are pious men. The standard of morality among the better class of society is very high."

The Harrisons were set to become residents of a thriving state. Hoosier newspapers were confident of the future, with one proclaiming that no other "Western state . . . has more towns that are advancing with greater rapidity than those of Indiana," and touted its "enterprise and energy, in every pursuit." Fueled in part by the development of the railroad (the Madison and Indianapolis Railroad had been completed in 1847), Indianapolis, which had become the state capital just twenty-five years earlier, had seen its population grow from 4,000 in 1847 to approximately 8,000 in 1850 and nearly 15,000 by the middle of the decade. Civic leaders were soon referring to their city as the "Great Railroad Center of the West."

VIEW OF INDIANAPOLIS.

An 1854 bird's-eye view of Indianapolis as seen from the top of the Indiana Institute for the Blind. Churches, the Indiana Statehouse, and other important structures are pictured around the border.

As one historian noted, the state capital had become "a haven for ambitious young Middle Westerners and a center of opportunity for the state."

Harrison arrived in Indianapolis in April 1854, boarding at the Roll House while Caroline, pregnant with their first child, stayed with her parents in Oxford, Ohio. The young attorney established his practice in the city, helped financially by $800 he received from property he had inherited along with $500 from his father. Harrison's business cards stated that he would "give prompt attention to all business" entrusted to his care, including recovery of unpaid bills. His law practice floundered at first. A few months after his arrival Harrison wrote that he would feel "contented if only I had some business to occupy my attention, however trifling the profits might be." Whatever discouragement he felt, however, Harrison vowed to "never suffer myself to falter in my purpose. I have long since made up my mind that with God's blessing and good health, I would succeed, and I never allow myself to doubt the result."

On August 12, 1854, Caroline gave birth to the couple's first child, a son, Russell. Upon her move with the baby to Indianapolis, the Harrison family rented a modest home on the south side of Vermont Street. One of Harrison's last chores before going to work was to chop enough wood to fill the wood box. Finances were always a problem. "They were close times, I tell you," Harrison noted. "A five dollar bill was an event." He had one good friend through these tough times, Robert Browning, a local druggist, who believed in the young attorney. "When things were particularly tight," Harrison recalled, "I could go into his store and borrow $5 from the drawer. A ticket in its place was all that was required. Such friends make life worth living."

Harrison had other good fortune. His friendship with John L. Robinson, the U.S. marshal, resulted in an appointment as town crier, for which he received a daily salary of $2.50. He soon also found success in the courtroom. For his first appearance before an Indianapolis jury, a burglary case, Harrison addressed the members at night in a dingy courthouse illuminated only by a few candles. Preparing to read his remarks, he found that the one candle provided him gave off too little light to read his notes. In desperation, he abandoned his notes and spoke from memory, winning the sympathy of the jury and admiration from others of his profession. Harrison learned a lesson from this incident for future public speaking—to always be prepared and not to rely on reading from prepared remarks for his talks.

In 1855 Harrison formed a law partnership with William Wallace, who sought a partner to take care of the office while he campaigned for the Marion County clerk's office. Harrison had joined forces with a prominent name in the Hoosier State, as William was the son of former governor

David Wallace and the brother of Lew Wallace, who later rose to the rank of general in the Civil War and won fame as the best-selling author of the historical novel *Ben-Hur: A Tale of the Christ*. Introduced to Harrison by a mutual friend when the young lawyer had first come to the city, Lew recalled that Harrison was small in height and had gray eyes tinged with blue and light hair, stating that "He was modest in manner, even diffident; but he had a pleasant voice and look, and did not lack for words to express himself."

View of Harrison's first residence in Indianapolis, located on East Vermont Street.

William was impressed with how hard Harrison worked, giving to every case "the best of his skill and labor, so that he never went unprepared." Hard work, however, did not always result in financial success. "He was poor," Wallace said of Harrison. "The truth is, it was a struggle for bread and meat with both of us." They were fortunate to earn the trust of two out-of-state firms, one from New York and one from Boston, for collection work, and also small fees of anywhere from one to five dollars for preparing contracts, wills, and tax reports, and offering other legal advice.

Although John Scott had warned his son to stay out of politics, describing it as a "drug, which should never be found in a gentleman's library or parlor . . . and fit only to scent the beer house," and proclaiming that "none but knaves should ever enter the political arena," its attractions were too much to resist. After all, Harrison was resident of a state where politics was viewed as a sport in which all eligible voters (males until the 1920s) should engage. As one of Harrison's biographers pointed out, a man's devotion to his party "became almost a religion; party discipline, an eleventh commandment." Harrison had gotten a taste for campaigning when William had run for the clerk position, making his first appearance in Acton, Indiana, before a crowd of approximately twenty spectators.

Beginning with William Henry Harrison's 1840 "Log Cabin—Hard Cider" presidential campaign and continuing through the 1940s, the Hoosier State played an important role in national politics. As an important "swing state" in national elections, Indiana often supplied candidates—presidents and vice presidents—to the country's major political parties, and "third parties" as well. In addition, from the adoption of its 1851 constitution through the 1880 election, Indiana was an "October state," casting ballots for state and local offices a month before national elections in November. Politics and literature seemed so essential to the Hoosier character that humorist Frank McKinney "Kin" Hubbard, through his cracker-barrel character Abe Martin, declared that everyone in

Woodcut for the Whig Party's log-cabin presidential campaign of 1840, with William Henry Harrison, in shirtsleeves, welcoming two soldiers with drinks of hard cider.

the state "is either a politician or writer. Of course there's a fair sprinkling of tradesmen an' farmers, but only enough t' supply the wants of the writers and politicians."

Harrison seemed to be a natural supporter of the Whig Party, the party of his father and grandfather. By the election of 1852, however, as the issue of slavery's expansion beyond the South became a central question, the Whig Party began to disintegrate. For the 1856 presidential election, Harrison threw his support to the new Republican Party, its candidate,

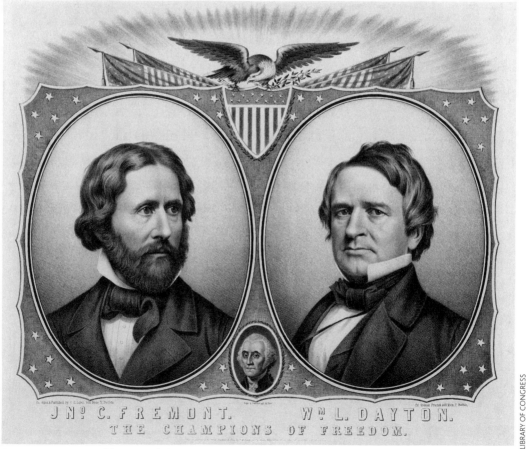

Banner touting Republican candidates John C. Frémont and William L. Dayton, produced for the 1856 presidential campaign. At the bottom is an oval portrait of President George Washington.

John C. Frémont, and the party's antislavery stance. Harrison's father had moved from the Whig Party to the now forgotten American Party and its presidential nominee, Millard Fillmore, in an election ultimately won by Democratic Party candidate James Buchanan. Harrison had made speeches on behalf of Frémont in Indianapolis and was determined to remain a Republican. "Our creed is plain," said Oliver P. Morton, who had been defeated as the party's candidate for governor. "We do not assail slavery where it exists entrenched behind legal enactments, but wherever it sallies forth, we are pledged to meet it as an enemy of mankind."

In 1857 Harrison ran and won on the Republican ticket for city attorney of Indianapolis, a job that offered a yearly salary of $400. After his one-year term ended, he considered running for the state legislature, but instead accepted a job as secretary of the Republican State Central Committee, becoming better known to fellow party members and its leaders around Indiana. Also in 1858 Harrison and Caroline welcomed the birth of their second child, a daughter, Mary.

In December 1859 Harrison made another run for public office, seeking the Republican nomination for the post of reporter for the Indiana Supreme Court, a job that involved gathering the court's opinions and seeing that they were published. He won the nomination against two other contenders and faced off in the 1860 campaign against Democrat Michael Kerr.

Still relatively unknown outside of Indianapolis, Harrison had some trouble during his first campaign event, scheduled for Lebanon in Boone County. Most of the crowd had gathered to hear Caleb B. Smith, known for his skill at speech making. When Smith finished his remarks, most of the crowd started to leave. Harrison's words, however, stopped them in their tracks. According to a newspaper account, the crowd, upon hearing his "terse and rugged sentences," began to return, "drop into their seats, or lean against some of the trees. Those who had got some distance away looked back and saw the deserted seats being filled up, and they, too, came back."

Harrison took a strong antislavery stand during his campaign. Taking a page from the great Whig politician Henry Clay of Kentucky, Harrison, during his speeches, vowed: "As long as God allows the vital current to flow through my veins, I will never, never, by word or thought, by mind or will, aid in admitting to one rood of Free Territory the Everlasting Curse of Human Bondage." When the ballots were counted on October 9, Harrison had won by 9,688 votes. For the November election, he continued campaigning, earnestly advocating for Republican presidential candidate

For the 1860 election, the Republican Party nominated Abraham Lincoln for president and Hannibal Hamlin for vice president with the slogan, "The Union Must and Shall Be Preserved."

Abraham Lincoln, a man he viewed as a "great simple hearted patriot."
Lincoln went on to win the state in which he had lived from age seven to
twenty-one by approximately 15,000 votes, and won the presidency with
180 electoral votes.

Lincoln's ascendancy to the nation's highest office sparked a strong
reaction from the slave-holding Southern states, which threatened to
withdraw from the Union to preserve their right to hold people in bondage.
A month after the election, South Carolina became the first state to secede.
The country's fate was on the president-elect's mind when, on his way from
his home in Springfield, Illinois, to Washington, D.C., for his inauguration,
he stopped in Indianapolis on February 11, 1861. During his speech to the
crowd gathered to welcome him, Lincoln reminded them that "if the Union
of these states and the liberties of this people shall be lost it is but little to
any one man of fifty-two years of age, but a great deal to the thirty millions
of people who inhabit these United States, and to their posterity in all
coming time. It is your business to rise up and preserve the Union and
liberty for yourselves, and not for me."

Harrison, who heard Lincoln speak, noted that it was a somber
occasion, remarking, "it seemed to me hardly to be a glad crowd, and he
not to be a glad man." Reflecting on what he had experienced that day,
Harrison later contemplated that the course before Lincoln seemed to be
"lighted only by the lamp of duty; outside its radiance all was dark. He
seemed to be conscious of all this, to be weighted by it, but so strong was
his sense of duty, so courageous his heart, so sure was he of his own high
purposes and motives . . . that he moved forward calmly to his appointed
work; not with show and brag, neither with shrinking."

Lincoln needed all the calm he could muster. Following South Carolina's
example, other Southern states soon left the Union. On February 18,
1861, Jefferson Davis, a former U.S. senator, was inaugurated as the new

A Harper's Weekly *illustration depicting the bombardment of Fort Sumter by Confederate artillery,* *April 12–13, 1861.*

president of the Confederate States of America. At 4:30 a.m. on April 12, 1861, Confederate forces started the American Civil War by firing on Fort Sumter, a Union military base located outside the entrance to the harbor at Charleston, South Carolina. Just two days later, after suffering severe damage from 4,000 shells, the federal forces surrendered. The American flag came down, and the Confederacy's Stars and Bars banner flew over the fort.

In Indianapolis Harrison had returned to his job as Indiana Supreme Court Reporter and collected enough material to publish the first volume of his reports. He was working on an index for the work in the basement of the First Presbyterian Church when he heard about the firing on Fort

Sumter. He could not know it at the time, but he was about to embark on quite a different activity than that for which he had been trained—the life of a soldier for the Union. It would be a life in which he strove, as he told Caroline, to bear himself as "a good soldier of Jesus Christ." He hoped to "conduct myself so as to honor my country and my friends," and, finally, "if consistent with His holy will . . . be brought 'home again' to the dear loved ones."

3

A Soldier for the Union

The attack on Fort Sumter, and the rush by Southern states to flee the Union to protect slavery, caused those in the North to rally quickly to preserve the United States. President Abraham Lincoln called for 75,000 volunteers to enlist for ninety days to meet the national emergency. "We must fight now," declared the *Indianapolis Journal*, "not because we want to subjugate the South . . . but because we *must*." Each Northern state worked to fill its quota of soldiers called for by the president. Indiana planned to fill the ranks of six regiments, about 4,600 men. "Soldiers, or good men willing to be converted into soldiers for the emergency," noted one Hoosier newspaper, "seem to spring up out of the ground, eager to protect the flag and conquer the peace."

Lew Wallace, a veteran of the Mexican War, was appointed by Governor Oliver P. Morton as the state's adjutant general, in charge of raising the needed number of troops. Just four days after Lincoln's call for volunteers, Wallace had managed to raise twice the number needed. "They were farmer boys, apprentice lads, leaders in villages, heads of public schools," Wallace said of the volunteers, "with here a city-born, and there a college-bred, and nearly all of them in the morning of life." Wallace, who took command of the Eleventh Indiana Volunteer Infantry Regiment, was careful to warn the recruits of what confronted them. As one Waveland, Indiana, recruit, Thomas Wise Durham, recalled, Wallace told him and the other men that

PATRIOTS YOUR COUNTRY NEEDS YOU!

THE UNION FOREVER!

Wanted--25 Men

To fill the ranks of the "INDIANA SNAKE KILLERS," in Colonel Scribner's Regiment at Camp Noble, New Albany.

Enquire of *A.B. Mighton W. Harvey 80*
Alter—

Camp Noble, Aug. 30th, 1861.

JOHN SEXTON, Captain,
JOHN CURRY, 1st Lieutenant,
G. W. WINDELL, 2d Lieut.

RECRUITING

OFFICE.

BOUNTY LAND AND BOUNTY MONEY!!

The undersigned is Commissioned by Governor Morton to enlist a Company in the Fourth Congressional District, for the 68th Regiment, and to muster recruits into the service of the United States. Pay to commence as soon as names are enrolled.

All communications addressed as below, will be promptly responded to.

July 21, 1862.

LIEUT. MARSHALL P. HAYDEN,
Rising Sun, Ohio County, Ind.

Above and Opposite: Recruiting notices such as these rallied Hoosiers to join the Union cause at the outbreak of the Civil War, with regiments being raised in New Albany (top), Rising Sun (above), and Evansville (opposite).

SOLDIERS
Wanted.

FREEMEN OF INDIANA! *We are in danger! The War rapidly approaches our homes!*

The Rebel Army, Commanded by General Pillow, has invaded the neutral ground of Kentucky, and threatens to march, 30,000 strong, upon Indiana. For Indiana the traitors entertain a peculiar hatred, because she has turned out better soldiers, and more of them, than any other state in proportion to population,

TO PRESERVE THE UNION

and maintain the Constitution and the laws, and perpetuate the only truly free Government on earth.

Seven Companies, of 1 hundred and one men each, are wanted immediately at Camp Vanderburgh, near Evansville. Rally Freemen! Rally promptly around the Flag of our Country, for if you fold your hands, and say: "a little more sleep, and a little more slumber," you may awake to find your homes desolated, and your children wandering naked through the world, begging for food, and seeking where to lay their heads.

> Who for liberty and law,
> Freedom's sword would strongly draw,
> Freeman stand or freeman fa',
> Let him follow me.
> Who so base as be a slave,
> Who would fill a coward's grave,
> Who would be a traitor knave,
> Let him turn and flee,

A Company of not less than fifty will be received and subsisted whenever they present themselves. The field officers will be

JAMES G. JONES, Col.
CHARLES DENBY, Lieut. Col.
JAMES M. SHANKLIN, Major.

P. S. The Government pays the expenses of transporting men from their homes to Camp.

although many in the North believed the war would be over quickly, it would "not be over in three months or a year, but will be a long and bloody conflict." Wallace was right; by the war's end after four years of relentless fighting, 25,025 Hoosiers had given their lives for the Union cause (7,243 died during battle, while the majority fell victim to disease).

At the war's outbreak, Morton, the first native-born Hoosier to serve as the state's chief executive and a steadfast Lincoln supporter, called on Republicans and Democrats to abandon political partisanship. "We have passed from the field of argument to the solemn fact of war," said Morton. Both parties should strive to bring about an "era when there shall be but one party, and that for our country." Some members of the opposition responded to the governor's call, but many Democrats were suspicious of Morton's intentions and saw his growing power in office as a threat to individual liberty. Democrats were also united in keeping the conflict from becoming a war to free the slaves. In April 1861 both the Indiana House and Senate approved a resolution stating that troops from the state should not be used "in any aggression upon the institution of slavery or any other constitutional right belonging to any of the states."

As American citizens prepared to kill one another in staggering numbers, Benjamin Harrison continued to conduct his public duties as Indiana Supreme Court Reporter and worked hard at his law practice to keep his head above water financially. He and Caroline suffered a tragic loss when their third child, a daughter, died at birth in June 1861. Harrison's professional circumstances also underwent an upheaval, as he and William Wallace, in December, ended their partnership. Harrison began a new firm with William P. Fishback, opening their offices at 62 East Washington Street. "During the time I was his law partner he worked like a slave," Fishback said of Harrison, who came close to wrecking his health from overwork.

Union forces had their own difficulties early in the war. One of the few victories was provided by a Hoosier regiment, as Lew Wallace's Eleventh Indiana won a small skirmish against Confederate troops at Romney, Virginia, routing them from the town. By July 1862, with the war far from over and the Army of the Potomac driven away from the Confederate capital of Richmond, Virginia, by General Robert E. Lee's Army of Northern Virginia, Lincoln issued a call for 300,000 men to volunteer for a period of three years "to bring the war to a speedy and satisfactory conclusion." Morton responded by issuing a special proclamation that stated: "I therefore call upon every man, whatever may be his rank and condition in life, to put aside his business, and come to the rescue of his country." The governor went on to say no matter what a man's position, "he has no business or duty half so important to himself and family as the speedy and effectual suppression of the Rebellion."

Indiana's Civil War governor, Oliver P. Morton, went on after the conflict ended to serve in the U.S. Senate before his death on November 1, 1877.

On July 9 Harrison, with his former law partner William Wallace, met with Morton at the governor's office. "Gentlemen," Morton told the two men, "there is absolutely no response to Mr. Lincoln's last call for troops. The people do not seem to realize the necessities of the situation. Something must be done to break the spirit of apathy and indifference which now prevails."

Harrison answered the call, telling the governor that if he "could be of any service, I will go." At first Morton was reluctant to lose Harrison's services as supreme court reporter, and urged him to recruit a regiment and he would find someone to command it. Harrison refused to ask men to fight without going himself. "Very well; if you want to go, you can command the regiment," Morton responded. Although Harrison pleaded a lack of experience in military tactics, he eventually accepted an appointment from Morton as a second lieutenant to organize the thousand men needed to form the Seventieth Indiana Volunteer Infantry Regiment, with his old law partner becoming his first recruit.

An 1863 portrait of Benjamin Harrison in the uniform of an officer in the Union army.

Using his law office as his recruiting office, Harrison sent out an advertisement urging fathers to stop restraining "the ardor of your sons, whose patriotic impulses prompt them to aid our country in its hour of trials. Ladies, give the stout and hearty young men who caught your smiles, to understand that 'the brave alone deserve the fair.'" By July 22 Harrison had been promoted to the rank of captain.

On August 7 Morton promoted him to the rank of colonel in command of the Seventieth Regiment. Although Harrison possessed no military training, one Indianapolis newspaper seemed confident of his success as the regiment's commander, writing that he had "the requisite amount of energy and ability to apply himself to the new work before him, and with a little experience will master those details of drill and discipline so essential to the good management of a thousand men."

Well aware of his inexperience when it came to the military, Harrison used his own money to pay for an experienced drillmaster to come from Chicago to train his novice regiment before it left Indianapolis on August 13 for its first service in Bowling Green, Kentucky. To his wife, he later wrote that if he died, she should "let your grief be tempered by the consolation that I died for my Country & in Christ."

Those officers in the Civil War who had been trained at the U.S. Military Academy at West Point, New York, distrusted those such as Lew Wallace and Harrison who had initially received their appointments through political connections. Wallace was a former Democrat who dropped his party connection to support the Union cause, and Harrison had been a true-blue Republican. Harrison, like Wallace, did all he could to live up to the responsibility given him. He became a stern taskmaster to the men of the Seventieth. Reveille sounded at 5:00 a.m. followed by drill before breakfast and more drilling in the afternoon. He also made sure there were a number of opportunities to attend religious services. "We are enforcing a very strict discipline in the camp," Harrison wrote his wife, "and the Regiment is progressing very finely in the drill." Some of the civilians turned soldiers in one company were irritated by their commander's sternness—one officer complained that he treated "his inferiors like dogs." Harrison confided to Caroline that although his men might "*grumble* about the strictness of my discipline," he knew they had confidence in his abilities to lead them into battle.

Harrison later earned a well-deserved reputation as a commander who invariably displayed concern for his men's well-being. Samuel Merrill, a fellow officer in the Seventieth, remembered Harrison as someone "merciful" on the march, protesting against any "unnecessary haste. Frequently he would take the guns and accoutrements of some poor worn-out fellows and carry them before him on the saddle." The colonel also

An engraving by a Philadelphia printer depicting President Abraham Lincoln signing the Emancipation Proclamation, declaring that as of January 1, 1863, all slaves in the rebellious states "shall be then, thenceforward, and forever free."

often dismounted from his horse and walked, giving up his seat on behalf of a sick soldier, Merrill recalled. "He protected the private soldier from imposition by those in authority, as a father would his own children," Merrill said of his commander.

The Seventieth had its first taste of combat in September 1862 when it received orders to investigate a Confederate camp near Russellville, Kentucky. For this first engagement with the enemy, Harrison and approximately 500 men from his regiment received helpful intelligence from an African American rider about Rebel troops camped nearby. Skillfully deploying his forces, Harrison surprised the Confederates, who fled only to come under fire by another group of the colonel's men. Approximately thirty-five Confederates were killed to one casualty for the Seventieth. In addition, Harrison wrote Caroline that his troops "took the rebel camp, forty-five good horses, about fifty guns . . . a large number of saddles and other accoutrements too numerous to mention, besides a dozen prisoners." One of his only complaints was that his regiment displayed "a little too much eagerness to get into the fight."

While Harrison celebrated his regiment's victory, his Republican Party suffered major setbacks in Indiana. Morton had done whatever he could— by constitutional or other means—to support the Lincoln administration and retain Republican control in Indiana. He charged that the state was infested with individuals (many Democrats) whose loyalties were to the Confederacy. Morton also stated that such treasonable secret societies as the Knights of the Golden Circle and the Sons of Liberty were operating in the state. Those who opposed the governor's power and policies or offered criticism were treated as disloyal. As a means to head off any opposition, Morton suspended the writ of habeas corpus, an action that authorized military authorities to arrest ordinary citizens.

General Harrison poses with other Union army officers, including General William T. Ward (seated) and Colonel David Dustin.

The threats to individual liberties, along with a string of Union defeats on the battlefield, the imposition of a draft, and the delivery of Lincoln's preliminary Emancipation Proclamation (freeing slaves in rebellious states unless they rejoined the Union) in September, worked to hurt the Republican Party at the polls during the October 1862 election. The *Indianapolis Sentinel*, a Democratic newspaper, called the president's actions "a confession of weakness—an acknowledgement that twenty millions of white people, with every advantage on their side, can not conquer six millions of whites." For his part, Morton supported Lincoln's actions, labeling the proclamation "a stratagem of war." The Democratic Party went on to claim a sweeping victory in the state, winning firm control of the Indiana General Assembly and capturing a majority of congressional seats. With Harrison absent, Democrats were also able to get a court to agree that he had vacated his supreme court reporter job, and saw its candidate, Michael Kerr, win a special election to fill the position.

In early 1863 Harrison and the Seventieth guarded railroad lines in Tennessee. Preparing for future action, Harrison studied the art of war, reading such works as W. J. Hardee's *Rifle and Light Infantry Tactics*, the three volumes of Silas Casey's *Infantry Tactics*, Imre Szabad's *Modern War: Its Theory and Practice*, and General Antoine-Henri de Jomini's *The Political and Military History of the Campaign of Waterloo*. Meanwhile in Indiana, Democrats attempted through legislation to strip Morton's control of the state militia. To halt such an action, Republican legislators, hoping to prevent a quorum so legislation could not pass, abandoned Indianapolis and fled to Madison, Indiana. Without the necessary legislators to pass legislation, the session ended without the approval of any appropriation bills to fund state government. Instead of calling a special session to address the crisis, Morton relied on loans from banks and on aid from the federal government to keep the state financially solvent. The legislature did not meet again for two years.

As Hoosiers warred with themselves, Harrison finally had another opportunity to prove his worth on the battlefield. At the beginning of 1864, the Seventieth became part of the campaign to capture Atlanta, Georgia. The campaign was part of a new command structure, with General Ulysses S. Grant serving as general in chief and General William Tecumseh Sherman taking command in the Western theater of action. Sherman had charge of the 60,000 members of George Thomas's Army of the Cumberland, the 25,000 members of James B. McPherson's Army of the Tennessee, and 13,000 under John M. Schofield's Army of the Ohio. Grant ordered Sherman to go after the approximately 65,000 men under Confederate general Joseph E. Johnston "and to get into the interior of the enemy's country as far as you can, inflicting all the damage you can against their war resources." Rebel leaders knew that losing Atlanta to the enemy would be a catastrophe for their cause. Confederate president Jefferson Davis noted that the fall of Atlanta would "close up those rich granaries from which [General Robert E.] Lee's armies are supplied. It would give them [the Union] control of our network of railways and thus paralyze our efforts."

The men of the Seventieth were placed in the Twentieth Army Corps under the direction of General Joseph "Fighting Joe" Hooker, former commander of the Army of the Potomac. On his way through Georgia, Harrison wrote Caroline describing his appearance as he moved into battle on horseback: "In front of my saddle I have my blue coat rolled up and strapped on. The small cavalry saddle bags are filled to their utmost capacity . . . my little tin bucket for making tea, swings clattering by my side. About my person I have my sword and belt, cantine [canteen] and haversack. The bundle behind my saddle is so large that it is a straining effort to get my leg over it in getting on or off and when in the saddle I feel like one who has been wrapped up for embalming . . . it is *very* disagreeable."

LIBRARY OF CONGRESS

A Kurz and Allison lithograph depicting the Battle of Resaca in Georgia.

The discomfort Harrison felt in the saddle would be nothing compared to what he faced at Resaca, Georgia, on May 14 and 15. Johnston's army had constructed strong defenses around the town, and the terrain offered its own challenges, with hills, swamps, and ravines. On the eve of his first major engagement, Harrison wrote his wife that he was in good spirits, "though not at all insensible to grave responsibilities and risks which I must bear tomorrow. I am thinking much of you and the dear children and my whole heart goes out to you in tenderness and love and many earnest prayers. . . . If God gives me strength I mean to bear myself bravely, and come what will, so that you may have no cause to blush for me, though you should be forced to mourn."

On May 15 Harrison and the Seventieth were ordered to take a Rebel battery that had been hammering Union forces with its artillery. Attacking in a column formation against a Confederate position located on the side of a thickly wooded hill, the Seventieth overwhelmed the enemy in spite of fire that seemed likely to annihilate them. "The men moved on with perfect steadiness," Harrison noted in his official report of the action, "and without any sign of faltering up the hillside and to the very muzzles of the enemy's artillery, which continued to belch their deadly charges of grape and canister, until the gunners were struck down at their guns." Waving a sword in one hand and a pistol in the other, Harrison rallied his troops to go forward to take another Rebel position. With "a wild yell," the Union soldiers continued their onslaught, "striking down and bayoneting the rebel gunners," said Harrison, "many of whom defiantly stood by their guns until struck down." In the confusion, and under heavy fire from an enemy who had rallied, Union reinforcements rushing to aid Harrison heard someone yell, "Retreat, they are flanking

Aerial view of New Hope Church, Georgia, with railroad tracks, dirt roads, and a few buildings in the distance.

us," and began to retire downhill. "I strove in vain to rally my men under the enemy's fire on the hillside, and finally followed them to a partially sheltered place behind a ridge to our left . . . preparing to lead them again to the support of those who still held the guns we had captured," Harrison noted.

Harrison's men were able to hand off to another regiment the guns (four twelve-pound Napoleon cannons) they had captured, and the colonel received praise for his work at Resaca, with Hooker commending the charge as "very brilliant and successful." Impressed by his steadfastness and cool nature under fire, the men of the Seventieth dubbed their colonel "Little Ben," an affectionate nickname he kept for the rest of the war. He received praise for his actions in Indianapolis newspapers and also received a warm letter of congratulations from his father, John Scott Harrison, who

Battlefield view of Peach Tree Creek, Georgia.

Soldiers of General William Tecumseh Sherman relax in a captured Confederate fort during the campaign to capture Atlanta in 1864.

expressed his pride in his son winning distinction in his new profession. "I am glad that I have been able to show them all that I could hold a creditable place in the army as well as in civil life," Harrison wrote Caroline, "and that if not the most petted one in the family, its famous name is as safe in my keeping as in that of any who now bear the name. We must not however think too much of the praises of the newspapers, nor forget that to God who sustains me belongs all the honor."

In a one-month period during the Union's fight to take Atlanta, Harrison, now in charge of a brigade of regiments that included the Seventieth, had participated in more battles than his grandfather, William Henry Harrison, had fought during his lifetime. At New Hope Church,

Georgia, Harrison had his troops fix bayonets to attack the enemy's position. "Men, the enemy's works are just ahead of us, but we will go right over them. Forward! Double-quick! March!" he ordered. After a bloody action at Golgotha Church near Kennesaw Mountain on June 15—fighting where two or three of his men had their heads torn off down to their shoulders—Harrison pitched in to help with the wounded, as the brigade's surgeons had been scattered in the fighting. "Poor fellows!" Harrison said of the casualties who had taken shelter in a frame house. "I was but an awkward surgeon of course, but I hope I gave them some relief," he wrote Caroline. The colonel treated some "ghastly wounds," including pulling from a soldier's arm a "splinter five or six inches long and as thick as my three fingers." He also ordered tents to be torn up so the strips of cloth could be used to bandage the wounded.

Harrison's skillful leadership on the battlefield came in handy on July 20 at Peach Tree Creek in Georgia, when he strengthened and then reestablished a weakened Union line against a Confederate attack by General John Bell Hood. "Come on boys," he shouted to his troops, "we've never been licked yet, and we won't begin now. We haven't much ammunition, but if necessary we can give them the cold steel, and before we get licked we will club them down; so, come on."

A fellow Union officer said that but for Harrison's courage that day, the army might have been "cut in two, and at least one wing of it rolled up and badly shattered." A relieved Hooker shook Harrison's hand and promised, "Harrison, by God, I'll make you a Brigadier [general] for this fight." The promise of promotion did not go to Harrison's head, as he reflected that the confidence he had won from the "brave officers and men of my command" was worth much more than a brigadier's star, "though the public will of course look to the latter as the evidence of the former." Hooker did keep his promise, writing a letter of recommendation to Secretary of War Edwin

President Abraham Lincoln's box at Ford's Theatre in Washington, D.C.

Stanton. Harrison did not achieve the rank of brigadier general, however, until February 23, 1865.

On September 2 Union forces finally captured Atlanta. Sherman wired officials in Washington, D.C.: "Atlanta is ours, and fairly won." On September 12 Harrison left the front for the first time in two years to enjoy a furlough in Indianapolis. His trip was not without danger. The steamboat he traveled on came under fire from unknown figures on the Ohio River shoreline. A fellow passenger remembered seeing Harrison on deck "with a revolver in each hand . . . blazing away with great enthusiasm and vigor at the people on the shore." Safely home, he had little time to rest, as he had to report for "special duty" to Morton.

Harrison's mission involved campaigning for the 1864 Republican ticket —Lincoln for president, Morton for governor, and himself for supreme court reporter—and recruiting additional troops for the Union army. In October both Morton and Harrison won their races, and the Republicans regained control of the state legislature. In November Lincoln won a second term as president, carrying Indiana by approximately 20,000 votes over his Democratic opponent, former Union general George B. McClellan. In stumping for Lincoln, Harrison praised the president's decision to issue the Emancipation Proclamation, and pointed out how escaped slaves had bolstered the army's ability to defeat the Confederates, giving much more aid "to our cause than the entire brood of whining, carping Copperheads [Northern Democrats who opposed the war] who object, in the interest of treason, to the employment of the black men." If the worst happened and McClellan defeated Lincoln, Harrison warned that the Copperheads would strip the uniforms off of the backs of free blacks and ex-slaves then fighting in the Union army and send them back into bondage.

On November 8, the day after Lincoln's re-election, Harrison received orders to rejoin the fighting. On his way to join Sherman's army, travel delays caused him to be rerouted to Nashville, Tennessee, where he led a temporary brigade formed to help meet a possible Confederate counter-offensive. Bad weather hampered both armies, and also provided an opportunity for Harrison to once again display his concern for the average soldier. On picket duty, Richard M. Smock of Indianapolis remembered

The tattered battle flags of Harrison's Seventieth Regiment photographed just after the capture of Savannah, Georgia.

seeing a man approaching him from the officers' quarters—it was
Harrison, who had with him a large can of hot coffee. When he asked him
what he was doing, Harrison, according to Smock, said he was "afraid that
some of the pickets would freeze to death, and he knew some hot coffee
would help the men to keep alive" in what many considered to be the
one of the coldest winters on record. "He was the most welcome visitor I

*Units of the Twentieth Army Corps, Army of Georgia, tramp past Pennsylvania Avenue near the
Department of the Treasury as part of the Grand Review of the Armies in Washington, D.C., May 24, 1865.*

ever met," Smock recalled, "for I really believe I would have frozen before morning had not the coffee been brought."

On January 16, 1865, Harrison received orders to join his old command with Sherman, now in Savannah, Georgia. After a brief furlough in Indianapolis, Harrison traveled, accompanied by his family, to Savannah via New York. While stopped in Honesdale, Pennsylvania, the home of Caroline's sister and her family, Harrison came down with scarlet fever and was placed by doctors in quarantine. He finally rejoined Sherman's command on April 19 in Raleigh, North Carolina, ten days after Lee's surrender to Grant at Appomattox Courthouse. While in Raleigh Harrison learned of Lincoln's assassination by actor John Wilkes Booth on April 14 at Ford's Theatre in Washington, D.C. "For hours," Harrison recalled, "men wept, or were stunned, or stood gritting their teeth and demanding that the armistice be ended so there might be one last savage battle."

Before his discharge from the army on June 8, Harrison participated in one of the last grand spectacles of the war—the Grand Review of the Armies in Washington, D.C. The soldiers of Sherman's army, which included Harrison and the men of the Seventieth, marched proudly down Pennsylvania Avenue for review by Grant and President Andrew Johnson on the morning of May 24. "The highest honors are due to the men who bore the cartridge and the gun," Harrison said to his command before the parade. "What were your officers without you? Much pride as we may take in Sherman, it was Sherman's Army, and not Sherman, that accomplished the great work." During the march, Harrison could hear people call out his name—friends "of whom I could only recognize a few."

At the age of thirty-two, Harrison's career as a soldier had ended. The citizens of Indianapolis welcomed him home with a celebration on June 16 honoring four returning Indiana regiments—the Twenty-Second, Seventieth, Seventy-Fourth, and Eighty-Second. Morton honored the soldiers by noting that Napoleon Bonaparte's crossing of the Alps was nothing when compared to "Sherman's march to the sea, or Grant's Vicksburg campaign." Called upon to make a speech, Harrison chose to remember those who had not returned to the Hoosier State. "Many who went out with us are not here," he said. "We buried them in Southern soil, but thank God the great secession flag does not wave over them. They sleep in the soil of the great Republic." He also looked to the future, when the former soldiers of the Union would be leaders in business and politics. Although they did not mean to "monopolize" public office, Harrison, prophetically predicting campaigns to come, warned that if anyone who ran for office could "be shown to have been lukewarm in the good cause, the boys will brand him with the word written on the shoulders of played-out horses—'condemned.'"

4

The Road to the White House

In the winter of 1872, from his Point Farm at North Bend, Ohio, John Scott Harrison wrote a cautionary letter to his son. Since his return from fighting for the Union in the Civil War, Benjamin Harrison had reestablished his successful Indianapolis law practice and had become an important figure in Indiana's resurgent Republican Party. In his letter the senior Harrison had expressed his opinion against his son being "mixed up with and compelled to hear the disgusting and polluted political atmosphere that seemed to be wafted from one end of the union to the other—enveloping men of both political parties." He advised Benjamin to take a year off and travel with his family, "leaving all business and cares behind."

With Benjamin considering a run as the Republican candidate for governor of the Hoosier State, John Scott, the former congressman, knew that his advice might fall on deaf ears. If his son moved ahead with his political ambitions, John Scott said he would have to "throw away all sensitivities—and put in for your armor—the hide of a Rhinoceros—for barbed arrows will be hurled at you from all sides." A politician, he continued, like a boxer, had to expect to receive, as well as give, "hard blows. The purity of a man's life is no security against political attacks—but in most cases it will secure us from the baneful effects of these attacks 'for truth is might and will prevail.'"

John Scott offered sound advice for any politician from the Hoosier State in the late nineteenth and early twentieth century, a period that has become known as the Gilded Age, a term taken by historians from Mark Twain and Charles Dudley Warner's novel *The Gilded Age: A Tale of Today* (1873). As one historian noted, it seemed as if "everyone wanted to be a millionaire." It was also a time when Indiana played an important role in national politics, becoming, as U.S. Senator Daniel W. Voorhees termed it, the "Belgium of politics, the debatable land between great contending parties and opinions."

John Scott Harrison believed in his son, Benjamin's, political future, predicting to him in 1875 that "high political honors are in store for you in the future—no one doubts."

Managers of both parties used whatever means necessary to gain votes for their candidates, including enticing voters from out of state and offering cash or liquor in exchange for votes. The need to win just a few key states (for example, Indiana, New York, and Connecticut) meant that most who were eligible to vote did so, with turnout at approximately 78 percent in presidential elections. As political historian Charles W. Calhoun noted, "political participation went beyond merely showing up at the polls. Political clubs attracted enthusiastic members across the nation, not only in cities but in small towns and rural areas as well." In Indiana supporters of both parties offered as proof of their loyalty that they had "risked the penitentiary" on a candidate's behalf.

Indiana and New York had become "swing states," able to swing a presidential election to either party if won, in part because of the return to power of the Democratic Party in the South. Democrats enacted a series of racist laws, enforced by threats of violence from such terrorist organizations as the Ku Klux Klan, that kept African Americans from the polls and ensured white supremacy following the end of Reconstruction in the late 1870s. Harrison had feared such an occurrence and warned his fellow Union veterans to be aware of traitors who would, if they could, "sneak in upon you while you sleep, and steal away the fruits of this bloody contest."

Republican politicians became adept in their speeches to party faithful to remind them, "Not all Democrats were Rebels, but all Rebels were Democrats," adding that they should "vote as you shot." In their speeches to the party faithful, Republican candidates also "waved the bloody shirt," reminding voters of the blood spilled by Union soldiers in saving the United States and asking them to avenge their sacrifices. The term was based on an apocryphal story of a speech in Congress by a Massachusetts Republican, Benjamin Butler, who supposedly waved aloft the bloody shirt of a Northern man whipped by the Ku Klux Klan during Reconstruction. Oliver P. Morton, Indiana's governor during the Civil War and a U.S. Senator, went so far as to describe the Democratic Party "as a common sewer and loathsome receptacle, into which is emptied every element of treason North and South."

Candidates became used to seeing their character dragged through the mud in local newspapers, which proudly proclaimed their party allegiances not just on their editorial pages, but also in news reports. Political differences often resulted in fistfights, as one Hoosier political historian noted, and neighbors "would often refuse to recognize neighbors because of differences in political views." Passion ruled over reason, with many considering a member of the opposite party "not only in the wrong, but willfully so, because he desired to bring disaster upon his fellow men and upon his country." Voters were eager to display support for their party of choice, wearing ribbons and buttons, marching in torchlight parades, and gathering by the thousands to hear speeches by party officials and candidates.

Upon his return from the war, Harrison had told his wife, Caroline, that he did not wish to become "a slave to my business," but longed instead "for a life of quiet usefulness," a thought that had "been on my mind on the march, on my cot, and even in my dreams." He believed he could have run, and won, a race for Congress, but declined to do so because it would have taken him away from home for too long. Fine words, but Harrison's work ethic proved too strong. By 1867 he had collapsed from overwork on behalf of his law firm, where he shared cases with William Fishback and a new partner, Albert Gallatin Porter. John Scott often worried about his son's health, warning him not to work too hard at his law practice. "It is well to be attentive and diligent in business," he wrote his son, "but there is no point of labour beyond which it is neither profitable or safe to go." Harrison decided against running for re-election as Indiana Supreme Court Reporter, and gave only a few speeches for the 1868 presidential election that saw Republican candidate and former Civil War general Ulysses S. Grant defeat his Democratic opponent, Horatio Seymour of New York.

Two Hoosier legal cases took up much of Harrison's professional time in the late 1860s and early 1870s, one involving a sensational murder and the other a treasonous Hoosier Democrat. In both cases he used his considerable oratorical skills to sway juries to his side. On September 12, 1868, the bodies of Jacob and Nancy Jane Young (her body had been badly burned) had been discovered at Cold Spring on the west bank of the White

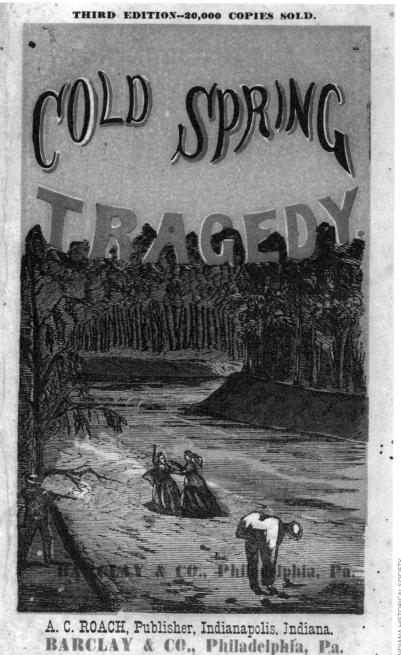

The cover of The Cold Spring Tragedy *imagined Nancy Clem pointing a pistol at Nancy Jane Young while Silas Hartman, Clem's brother, fires a shotgun at an unsuspecting Jacob Young.*

River northwest of Indianapolis in a scene a local newspaper described as "a picture of grisly horror seldom seen except upon the battle field." Authorities eventually charged Jacob Young's business partner, Nancy Clem, and two accomplices, including her brother, Silas Hartman, for the murders. The state engaged Harrison's law firm to help prosecute the accused, and Harrison played a vital role in Clem's second trial in February 1869, after a jury had failed to reach a verdict in the first trial.

As usual, Harrison prepared with great care, especially his final argument for the state's case, speaking for eight hours before the jury. He paid particular attention to the gruesome nature of Jane Young's death, harkening to the "bleached remains, charred until scarce a vestige of her image was left!" Harrison asked the jury to "remember the dead that are buried away out of sight; to remember the hearthstone whose fire has gone out forever. I ask you to remember that orphan child who is wandering fatherless and motherless to-day." The jury returned a verdict of guilty for all three defendants, and sentenced Clem to life in prison, whereby she became the first woman in Indiana to be convicted of murder. (The Indiana Supreme Court overturned the verdict, and although Clem was convicted a second time, she never served time in prison for the Cold Spring murders, but did spend time in jail for perjury in a separate case.) Indianapolis newspapers heaped praise upon Harrison for his skillful prosecution. "The road was mapped out from the beginning, and followed with a patience vigilance and energy that has added to the already high reputation of General Harrison," said an article in the *Indianapolis Journal*.

The second sensational case that boosted Harrison's standing with the public involved a Hoosier, Lambdin P. Milligan, who, along with other conspirators, planned an armed uprising in Indiana during the Civil War that involved freeing and arming Confederate prisoners in Indianapolis.

The plot was thwarted and Milligan and the others were tried by a military commission, found guilty, and sentenced to death. On appeal, however, the U.S. Supreme Court in a landmark case, *Ex parte Milligan*, decreed that trying citizens in a military court while civilian courts were still functioning was unconstitutional.

In 1868 Milligan sued those involved in his arrest and trial, including General Alvin P. Hovey and former governor Morton, seeking $500,000 in damages for defaming someone who had been, he said, "an innocent, Union-loving citizen." When the case went to trial in the U.S. Circuit Court for the District of Indiana in May 1871, President Grant called upon Harrison to defend Hovey, Morton, and the others. By this time Milligan had reduced his damage claim to $100,000. "The trial excited great public interest," noted Lew Wallace, himself a former Union general, "as at that time the echoes of the war were still distinctly heard." Of particular interest were the two contending counsels—Harrison for the defense and former Democratic congressman Thomas A. Hendricks (and future governor and vice president) on Milligan's behalf. Harrison cleverly managed to enter into evidence the treasonable actions of Milligan and his associates—villains of "blacker hue than those whom the law from day to day is putting its hands upon in our criminal courts." He compared their treasonous behavior to that of the patriotic actions of the defendants. "They were United States soldiers who had heard the cry of national distress," Harrison told the jury, "and with brave, true hearts, had forsaken all and dared all, that they might preserve us as a nation." The lawyer's words struck home and, although Milligan won the case, the jury awarded him only five dollars in damages.

The time seemed ripe for Harrison to seek another elected office, and his name drew attention as a possible candidate for the Republican nomination for governor in 1872. Two things stood in his way. Morton, now a U.S. Senator, and his supporters controlled the Republican Party in the state, and were cool to Harrison, seeing him as a potential threat. In addition, as potential candidates jockeyed for support before the Republic state convention in Indianapolis in February 1872, Harrison declined to do any personal campaigning. His inaction led to rumors being circulated by his opponents that he was "as cold-blooded as a fish" and far too "aristocratic" in character to appeal to common Hoosiers. Harrison, who believed it improper for a candidate to "open headquarters and solicit support," later admitted that his friends had "complained of me for manifesting so little personal interest in the result." At the convention, Harrison lost the nomination to Thomas M. Browne, who lost the governor's race by 1,148 votes to Hendricks.

Exterior of the Harrison home on North Delaware Street with its picket fence.

More personal matters occupied Harrison's attention after his political disappointment, especially the building of a new home for his family. In May 1868 Harrison purchased a double lot on the west side of North Delaware Street, with construction on the structure beginning two years later. After spending approximately $25,000, the Harrisons moved to the sixteen-room, Italianate-style home designed by architect Herman T. Brandt. The three-story, red-brick house had such rare conveniences for the day as a coal-fed furnace; running water in its kitchen and bathroom; twelve-foot-high ceilings; twenty-three gaslights; and a burglar alarm of bells and strings attached to doors. Surrounding the property was 153 feet of picket fencing. The library featured a steel engraving of Harrison's

BENJAMIN HARRISON PRESIDENTIAL SITE

The library at the Harrison Home. Note the sword leaning against the bookcase at the right of the photograph.

grandfather, President William Henry Harrison. Except for his residence in the White House, Benjamin Harrison remained in his comfortable north-side Indianapolis home for the rest of his life.

In 1876 the forty-two-year-old Harrison returned to the political fray, though not by any efforts of his own making. With Morton still firmly in control of Indiana Republicans, Harrison had shied away from taking any part in his party's choice for governor, which had gone to Godlove S. Orth, a former congressman. Democrats nominated James D. Williams, a veteran state legislator and former congressman known by the nickname "Blue Jeans" for his habit of wearing suits of denim fabric made by his wife from wool from his own sheep. Williams had earned a reputation as a man of the people, someone accustomed to the ups and downs of farm life and honest in his

Hoosier Democratic politician James D. "Blue Jeans" Williams served in the Indiana General Assembly from 1844 to 1872 before his election as governor.

dealings with others, as well as a man who knew the value of a dollar and seemed reluctant to part with one. Democratic partisans used Williams's homespun charm and manner to good effect in the election.

Hounded by rumors that he had been involved in shady financial dealings involving Venezuela, and losing the support of Morton, Orth, on August 2, withdrew from the race. Panicked Republican officials turned to Harrison, a "man of integrity," to save the party from disaster on Election Day, set for October 10. After all, a strong showing by the Hoosier Republican candidate for governor might well help the party's presidential candidate, Rutherford B. Hayes, in his race against Democrat Samuel J. Tilden in November. Party officials telegrammed Harrison, who was returning from a vacation trout fishing at Lake Superior. The message read: "The Central Committee and Republicans throughout the state demand your candidacy for governor. They feel that this is a time when you should sacrifice private interest for public good. Your friends who justified your declination before now think that you should accept." Large partisan crowds met him at train stations in Muncie and Indianapolis, beseeching him to enter the race.

Refusing to be stampeded into a hasty decision, Harrison took a few days before deciding to accept the offer and run for governor. He knew it would not be an easy campaign, as a financial panic in 1873 and corruption in Grant's administration had weakened Republican chances of victory. In addition, Harrison had to contend with another competitor for the governorship, Anson Wolcott, the candidate of the newly formed Independent Greenback Party, taking its name from "greenbacks," the paper currency printed during the Civil War and not backed by reserves of gold or silver. The issuance of such currency might lead to higher inflation, which could, the party believed, help farmers to pay off their debt. Most Republicans, especially those living on the East Coast, backed a return to gold-based currency, "sound money," while Democrats' views often depended on the region of the country they were from. Harrison was a "sound money" supporter, believing such a stand favored "the poor man, the laboring man—the men who are most liable to be deceived by those who have better opportunities for information in regard to matters of finance."

At a speech in Morgan County, Harrison, the Civil War veteran, proudly accepted what he called "the banner of the bloody shirt." He hammered away at the Democratic Party, indicating that Republicans would continue to campaign on the issue, taking as their "ensign the tattered, worn-out, old gray shirt, worn by some gallant Union hero, stained with his blood as he gave up his life for his country." When the Democrats decided to "purge their party of the leprosy of secession," then would Republicans "bury the 'bloody shirt' in the grave with the honored corpse who wore it and not before."

Late in the race, Wolcott withdrew, and threw his support to Harrison (The Greenbackers substituted a new candidate, Henry W. Harrington). When the ballots were counted, Harrison lost to Williams by a vote of 213,219 to 208,080. Harrison blamed his defeat on Wolcott's last-minute endorsement. "The fact that he withdrew in my favor at the 11th hour gave rise to the suspicion in the minds of many that there was a monied inducement, and the time was too short to convince them to the contrary," he said. Democrats were also able to portray Harrison to voters as out of touch with the average Hoosier, comparing the two candidates as "blue jeans" (Williams) and "blue blood" (Harrison). Republicans did not place any personal blame on Harrison for the defeat. The *Indianapolis Journal*, which supported the Republican cause, went as far as to claim that Harrison's reputation with the entire country was "infinitely superior to that occupied by his successful competitor," and he had "won the lasting gratitude of the party and a secure place in the affections of all its members."

Tamping down his disappointment at his loss, Harrison took to the stump to campaign on behalf of Hayes, the eventual presidential winner, in the critical states of New Jersey and Pennsylvania in October. While covering a speech by Harrison, a reporter for the *Philadelphia Times* produced a riveting portrait of the Hoosier politician for a national audience. The reporter wrote of Harrison:

> He is about 5' 6" in height and slenderly built. A well-formed head rests upon a square set of shoulders. The face of the General is adorned

by a full, light brown beard, cut close, and a heavy mustache appears under his shapely nose. The forehead is of medium height and retreats to a luxuriant mass of light hazel-colored hair, slightly tinged with gray. A pleasant pair of little blue eyes and a clear cut mouth complete the picture of the orator. . . . While speaking he is all energy, nervous and wiry, gesticulates rapidly, putting a full point to each sentence with a rapid motion of clenched fists. It cannot be said that he is an eloquent speaker; his forte seems to be clean enunciation, rapid delivery and emphasis.

Harrison's loss to Williams might have seemed like a blessing in disguise, as early in his term in office Indiana's new governor had to deal with a major labor crisis that crippled Indianapolis for a time. As one of the city's leading citizens, Harrison soon found himself deeply engaged in the

A Harper's Weekly *illustration showing the blockade of railroad engines at Martinsburg, West Virginia, during the Great Strike of 1877.*

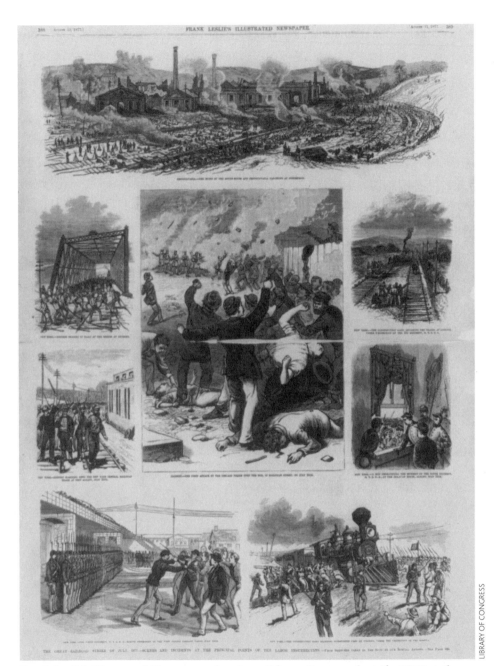

Frank Leslie's Illustrated Newspaper *drawings of dramatic scenes from the 1877 strike included rioters marching down the New York Central tracks at West Albany, New York; soldiers protecting workmen repairing tracks at Corning, New York; and a mob threatening troops taking possession of the West Albany, New York, freight yards.*

crisis as well. In the summer of 1877 railroad workers across the country went on strike for better wages and working conditions, paralyzing railroad freight traffic in what became known as the Great Strike of 1877. Violence broke out in West Virginia, Maryland, and Pennsylvania as workers clashed with units of state militia, with some deaths occurring. Eventually, President Hayes sent federal troops to Maryland, the first time such forces had been used to stop a strike in peacetime.

In Indianapolis local newspapers kept a close eye on railroad workers, noting that they were "working themselves up into a fever and are rapidly approaching a point from which it will be an easy matter to jump into a general strike," which occurred on July 23. Mayor John Caven strove to keep the city peaceful, signing up strikers as special police officers, asking for taverns and salons to close, and beseeching residents to organize against thieves or others who might take advantage of any disturbance. Williams also was reluctant to call out the state militia or ask for federal troops, fearing such moves would backfire and incite violence.

Fearing that the mayor and governor had done too little to safeguard Indianapolis, some of the city's leading citizens, including Harrison and federal judge Walter Q. Gresham, worked together to form a Committee of Public Safety to organize residents into an emergency militia. Harrison even sent a telegram to officials in Washington, D.C., indicating he could provide 200 men to guard federal property if the need arose, and stood ready to return to his role as an officer to command them. He opposed, however, direct action by the militia against the workers. "I don't propose to go out and shoot down my neighbors when there is no necessity for it," he said. He became part of a Committee of Mediation that met with the strikers to hear their complaints, agreeing with them that their wages were inadequate, but also arguing that businessmen had been hurt by their illegal strike. At meetings with the workers Harrison urged them to follow the law and avoid violence. If they did so, he would use his influence on their behalf. "Citizens will not tolerate mob rule, it has been tried again and again," he told them. "The sooner you realize that you are breaking the laws of the land . . . the sooner you will regain the sympathy and confidence of the public and gain your ends."

The strike ended in late July with no violence in Indianapolis or elsewhere in the state. Although most of his fellow citizens had nothing but praise for Harrison's actions during the affair, there was a lingering feeling from some that he did not support labor. His political opponents used these vague suggestions that he was antiworker against him in subsequent campaigns. Democrats charged, unfairly, that Harrison during the 1877 strike had said that "a dollar a day is enough for any workingman," and invented a ridiculous story that an irate Harrison had confronted striking railroad workers and said: "I would force you to work by the bayonet, or I would shoot you down like dogs."

Harrison believed that his stance in favor of tariffs, or protectionism, actually favored workers in the long run. (Tariffs are taxes placed on imported goods in order to protect domestic industries.) "The cry of the free trader is for a cheaper coat, an English coat," Harrison said, "and he does not seem to care that this involves a cheapening of the men and women who spin, and weave, and cut, and stitch."

On November 1, 1877, Morton, longtime leader of the Republican Party in Indiana died, opening the door for Harrison to take his place. Harrison also attracted the attention of national Republican officials, who were impressed by his steadfast support of a party he believed "represented the moral conscience of the people of the nation," and one that always "sympathized with and aided the efforts of every class of people who were seeking a larger liberty and a more perfect sphere for the development of their powers." Harrison's rise to political prominence, however, was tempered by the loss of one of his biggest supporters, his father, John Scott, who died on May 25, 1878, at North Bend, Ohio. Harrison's grief was compounded by a shocking incident that befell his family—the theft of his father's body by grave robbers, who were a scourge in the late 1800s, selling bodies to medical schools eager to have them so students could practice dissection. Those attending John Scott's burial had noticed that a nearby gravesite—that of Augustus Devin, a young cousin of the Harrisons—had been robbed. The Harrison family took measures to guard against the same thing happening to them, reinforcing their father's grave and hiring someone to guard the site for the next month.

These precautions did not work. When Harrison's brother, John, and one of his cousins searched for Devin's stolen body at the Medical College of Ohio, they were shocked to instead find John Scott's body there (Devin's corpse was later discover at the University of Michigan). Medical school authorities were unremorseful about the theft, prompting Harrison to file a civil suit against the school and to publish a letter lambasting it, noting, "While he [John Scott] lay upon your table, the long white beard, which the hands of infant grandchildren had often stroked in love, was rudely shorn from his face. Have you so little care of your college that an unseen and an unknown man may do all this?" The outcome of the lawsuit is lost to history. An 1884 fire destroyed the Hamilton County Courthouse in Ohio, and the records concerning Harrison's lawsuit were destroyed.

By the time of the 1880 Republican National Convention, Harrison had attracted enough support that there was some talk of him snatching the presidential nomination if delegates could not agree on a choice, or being selected as a vice presidential candidate. As head of the Indiana delegation, Harrison used his power to swing the state's support to a compromise candidate, Ohio's James A. Garfield, a Civil War general and congressman, over his more well-known rivals, including former president Ulysses S.

Grant and Senator James G. Blaine. After Garfield defeated his Democratic opponent, Winfield Scott Hancock, speculation grew that Harrison might be offered a position in the president-elect's cabinet. Instead, Harrison, with Republicans in control of the Indiana legislature, decided to run for the U.S. Senate seat being vacated by Democrat Joseph E. McDonald. (The party controlling a state legislature had the authority to pick a state's two senators until passage of the Seventeenth Amendment to the U.S. Constitution in 1913. The amendment provided for the popular election of senators.) "I have made up my mind to be a candidate for the Senate," Harrison wrote Garfield. "There are four or five others in the field who are very busy—still, I think I shall succeed."

Harrison's main competition for the Senate seat, Gresham, as well as two former congressmen (Will Cumback and Goodlove Orth), faded from consideration and, on January 18, 1881, the Indiana legislature selected Harrison as the state's new senator. Although Garfield still wanted the man from Indiana for his cabinet, Harrison choose to serve in the Senate, and on March 4 he was sworn into office for a six-year term to a body that had thirty-seven Democrats, thirty-seven Republicans, and two independents. (After Garfield's assassination, his successor, Chester Alan Arthur, appointed Gresham as his postmaster general.) Later, writing to a friend, Harrison expressed his

Although a Republican for most of his life, Walter Q. Gresham, in 1893, served as Secretary of State in Democrat Grover Cleveland's administration.

pride at winning his position by campaigning on a "high plane . . . no living man can say that I promised anything for his support, or suggested any motive to influence him that was not consistent with his honor and mine." He added that there were still many things about a life in politics that he found "distasteful," noting many times he could only find it possible to "do second or third best . . . instead of the first as I would like."

During his time as a senator in Washington, D.C., Harrison earned the respect of his fellow Republicans as a hard worker and plunged into legislative battles that reappeared during his presidency. These included tariff policy, the federal budget surplus, increased pensions for Civil War veterans, protection of voting rights for African Americans in the South, increased federal support for education, improvements to the country's naval forces, possible statehood for the southern portion of the Dakota Territory, and setting aside the Grand Canyon as a public park (it became a national park in 1919).

Although advocating government spending, Harrison did so while also believing that giveaway programs were wrong and such efforts "should always be so regulated as to save self-respect and awaken in the mind of the recipient a lost faith in his ability to take care of himself. We should carefully avoid that giving which creates a disposition to lean and to expect, which takes the stamina and strength and self-dependence and industry out of men." The tariff question, present since the earliest days of the Republic, remained divisive. Harrison and his fellow Republicans opposed Democratic attempts to reduce tariffs, fearing competition from foreign manufacturers.

As he had with his law practice, Harrison faithfully kept to his responsibilities as senator, and they sometimes weighed on his mind and spirit. "Life here is slavish to those who feel like conscientiously trying to do their duty," he wrote a friend. "You know I used to be a hard worker at

BENJAMIN HARRISON PRESIDENTIAL SITE

Looking to the 1888 presidential race, one of his friends noted that while Harrison was not a candidate, he had "good reason to believe he will listen to the advice of his friends."

home but I usually had my evenings for rest. Here I have no time out of bed that is my own, and bed time is very late, which you know must be a great grief to me." Especially irksome were the numerous pleas he received from Republican Party supporters for patronage jobs in government, a task he found burdensome. "I covet for myself the free and unpurchased support of my fellow-citizens," Harrison said, "and long to be able to give my time and energy solely to . . . public affairs."

The 1884 presidential election saw Harrison engaged in a heated battle with Gresham over the support of Indiana's delegation to the Republican convention in Chicago. Both men gave way to the eventual nominee, Blaine, who would go on to lose the election to his Democratic opponent, Grover Cleveland. In addition to contending with an unfriendly president, Harrison found his hopes at securing another term in the U.S. Senate dashed when Democrats controlling the Indiana General Assembly redrew state legislative districts in their favor—an effort Harrison labeled as "A Bill to Prohibit the Election of a Republican United States Senator from Indiana." He was right; in 1886 Democrats selected one of their own, David Turpie, to replace Harrison.

In defeat Harrison had still managed to garner much goodwill among his fellow Republicans, especially for his tireless campaigning on the party's behalf throughout the country. In his speeches he had warned voters against letting the Democrats win, passing control of the government held by Republicans "into the hands of the Solid South and their northern allies." The Hoosier politician looked more and more like a strong possibility to be the Republican nominee for president in 1888, and then to put the party back in control of the White House—something Harrison sought even if he was not the candidate. For Harrison the Civil War remained a raw memory. As he told party members in a March 1888 speech in Chicago, Republicans had taken the "ship of state when there was treachery at the helm, when there was mutiny on the deck, when the ship was among the rocks, and we put loyalty at the helm; we brought the deck into order and subjection." He foresaw that the "great party of 1860 is gathering together for the coming election with a force and a zeal and a resolution that will inevitably carry it . . . to victory in November."

5

The 1888 Election: Harrison versus Cleveland

A young reporter for the *Indianapolis News*, Hilton U. Brown, found himself in an enviable position on June 25, 1888—one that any journalist in America would have coveted. Brown had been one of about ten people gathered inside Benjamin Harrison's law office on Market Street in Indianapolis. They were waiting to hear news from the Republican National Convention in Chicago. Harrison was under consideration to be his party's candidate for the presidency against Democratic incumbent Grover Cleveland. The *News* reporter was there when Harrison, huddled near the telegraph ticker, finally received a message from Louis T. Michener, his political adviser: "You are put in command."

The news threw the office into commotion. According to Brown's account in his autobiography, those in the room shouted their congratulations to Harrison and one of the "ladies present in her exuberant enthusiasm threw her arms around the General [Harrison] and gave him a hearty smack," saying to him, "Oh general, I am so glad." For his part, the new presidential nominee was initially composed enough to acknowledge the cheers of the crowd, which had gathered on the streets below with cries of "What's the matter with Harrison?" followed by the refrain, "He's all right!" His emotions nearly overcame Harrison afterward and one report indicated "he nearly fainted and had to lie down." Harrison's secretary, Frank Tibbott, quickly ran the ten blocks to his boss's Delaware

Entrance to the law office of Benjamin Harrison, William H. H. Miller, and John B. Elam, Wright's Block, Indianapolis.

Street home to prepare for the candidate's homecoming.

At the house, enthusiastic spectators had already begun to tear pieces from the white picket fence that surrounded the property (it would eventually be picked clean). The gathering throng in her front yard had alerted Caroline Harrison that something momentous had occurred. Newspaper accounts had her commenting to her daughter, "Well . . . your father's got it [the nomination]." After witnessing some of the damage done to her home by souvenir hunters, Caroline was alleged to have said to a friend, "One thing is certain, either we'll live in the White House or we'll have to go to the poorhouse."

Upon his arrival home, Harrison, was greeted by a cheering crowd of his neighbors and friends. From the stoop of his home, Harrison gave the first of what were to be several speeches he would make from Indianapolis, telling the crowd gathered before him the following:

> Kings sometimes bestow decorations upon those whom they desire to honor, but the man is most highly decorated who has the affectionate regard of his neighbors and friends. I will only again thank you most cordially for this demonstration of your regard. I shall be glad from time to time, as opportunity offers, to meet all personally, and regret tonight that this crowd is so great that it will be impossible for me to

take each one of you by the hand but we will be here together and my house will always open its doors gladly to any of you when you may desire to see me.

The journey to the nomination for Harrison had been one that most contemporary politicians, used to years-long struggles for their party's top prize, would not recognize. In 1888 Harrison ran in no statewide primaries seeking the delegates necessary for victory at the convention. Instead, he relied on the friends he had made from his steady schedule of speeches before party members, and especially on his relatively good relationships with top Republican officials who knew the party needed Indiana's fifteen electoral votes if it wanted to win the presidency. In public Harrison

BENJAMIN HARRISON PRESIDENTIAL SITE

Indianapolis residents rushed to Harrison's home to offer their congratulations upon learning of his nomination as the Republican Party's presidential candidate in 1888.

A delegation from Danville, Indiana, who traveled to the Harrison home to offer congratulations included a brass band, seen gathered at the center of the photograph.

downplayed any suggestions that he aspired to the country's top office, telling a friend that although "the thought had been with him many times when suggested by others," he "had never been possessed by it or had his life shaped by it." When Wharton Barker, a Philadelphia banker, urged him to seek the presidency in 1884, Harrison had objected, writing Barker, "I have never sought occasions for display or attempted to anything brilliant or for applause. A somewhat prosy—perhaps stupid—habit of trying to discharge quietly, but to my best, such few public duties as have been cast upon me is hardly likely to make of me 'Presidential timber.'" When the chance for the presidency presented itself in 1888, however, Harrison never flagged at grabbing the opportunity to gain the White House.

The presumptive nominee for the Republicans in 1888 seemed to be James G. Blaine, the party's standard-bearer four years before and someone who still had great support among rank-and-file Republicans, with his fans among them dubbed "Blainiacs." Blaine had been active in answering Cleveland's call to Congress in late 1887 for a reduction of the tariff ("What is the use of being elected or reelected unless you stand for something?" the president asked), saying such a move would only help create "an enlarged market" in America for British goods. Health problems, however, plagued Blaine, and he seemed reluctant to do battle again for his party's presidential nomination. "Ever since the result of 1884 I have made my mind up to run again if called upon by an undivided and unanimous party, but not to run again if a contest were required to secure my nomination," Blaine wrote a friend while on a tour of Europe. His withdrawal opened up the field to a variety of candidates, including

Maine politician and statesman James G. Blaine.

Senator John Sherman of Ohio (the brother of Civil War general William Tecumseh Sherman), and Harrison, with both representing states critical to Republican success in the November election. Other possibilities bandied about were Harrison's Hoosier rival Walter Q. Gresham, New York businessman Chauncey M. Depew, and former Michigan governor Russell A. Alger.

Although careful not to publically advocate on behalf of any of the contenders, behind the scenes Blaine seemed to view

Registered for copyright on the eve of the Republican convention in Chicago, this print reminded viewers of the Republican Party's first successful presidential candidate, Abraham Lincoln.

Harrison as his party's best choice. After all, Harrison had campaigned vigorously on Blaine's behalf in the 1884 election and represented Blaine when he sued the Democratic-supporting *Indianapolis Sentinel* for libel when it published lurid articles about his marriage. Blaine noted in a letter to one of his top advisers that "the one man remaining, who in my judgment can make the best run, is Ben Harrison." Still, Blaine harbored hope that his party would turn to him if it could not agree on a candidate.

Harrison begged off any public pronouncements on his candidacy, careful to keep friendly relations with Blaine, but he made sure his supporters controlled the Indiana delegation to the Republican convention and had representatives, especially Michener, ready to push his name with the delegates in Chicago. The delicate political balancing act worked; on the eighth ballot, Harrison captured the Republican presidential nomination.

Portraits of the 1888 Republican ticket, Harrison and Levi P. Morton of New York. After his one term as vice president, Morton went on to serve as New York's thirty-first governor.

INDIANA HISTORICAL SOCIETY

Before his election as the twenty-second president in 1884, Grover Cleveland had served as mayor of Buffalo, New York, and as New York's twenty-eighth governor.

Immediately after Harrison had gained the needed votes, an Ohio delegate asked that his nomination be made unanimous, saying, "Ohio came here all Sherman men. They are now all Harrison men." For the Hoosier Republican's running mate, the convention selected Levi P. Morton, a wealthy New York businessman and former congressman and ambassador.

American political tradition had called for presidential candidates to avoid getting their hands dirty grubbing for votes by doing actual campaigning. In 1884 Blaine had defied tradition and made numerous appearances, giving approximately four hundred short talks. One of these appearances—a stop in New York City in late October—might have cost him the election. In a welcoming address, a Protestant clergyman had noted: "We are Republicans, and don't propose to leave our party and identify ourselves with the party whose antecedents have been Rum, Romanism, and Rebellion," words that angered many Irish American Catholics in New York and elsewhere (Blaine lost to Cleveland by approximately 23,000 votes).

Republican officials wanted to avoid any reoccurrences of Blaine's blunder. And although Harrison was known to be a fine public speaker, he had no interest in barnstorming around the country to publicize his candidacy, preferring to remain home in Indianapolis. His friends and some Republican officials expressed concern that he not give the opposition any ammunition to use against his candidacy. "If you were under my command as of old," said Daniel Butterfield, a Union Civil War general, "I should say steady—no speeches—no letters—we will carry you through." The excitement of having one of their own running for the nation's highest office, however, inspired Hoosiers by the score to troop to Harrison's home to hear his words, and the candidate responded by pursuing a front-porch campaign similar, in part, to the one waged by successful Republican presidential candidate James Garfield in 1880.

Indianapolis residents unveil a banner supporting their Hoosier favorite son and his running mate for the 1888 presidential election.

Indiana—a state both parties needed to win—became a hotbed of activity. The city's central location and easy railroad access added to the ease by which Republican supporters could travel to meet their candidate. "I never in my life saw anything like it," Allen W. Thurman, the son of Democratic vice presidential candidate Allen G. Thurman, wrote Cleveland of the situation in the Hoosier State. "Men, women, and children, boys and girls, have all gone crazy on the subject of politics." Those too young to vote still wanted in on the fun. Encountering a group of thirty children while on a walk, Harrison heard them chant: "We are for Harrison, he is the man. If we can't vote, our daddies can."

While Cleveland remained in the White House, content with his duties as president and believing in the dictum "the office sought the man," Harrison embarked on a busy speaking schedule that saw him give more than eighty extemporaneous talks to more than 300,000 visitors to Indianapolis from July 7 to October 25. Usually, there were anywhere from one to three delegations per day, but at one point Harrison met seven on one day. To meet the demand posed by those who clamored to see the candidate at his Indianapolis home, a "committee of arrangements" was formed to manage the deluge of letters sent to Harrison and to schedule and control visitors.

The crowds soon overwhelmed the space at the Delaware Street house, and instead were moved about a mile away to University Park, the former drilling ground for Union soldiers. Marching bands were on hand at Union Station to welcome delegations as they arrived, and accompanied them as they walked to the park. All the remarks made by outside groups were closely scrutinized to ensure that no controversial statements were uttered, and Harrison listened to them and often adjusted his speech to reflect what had been covered. Delegations included such groups as Union war veterans, railroad workers, African American supporters, young girls who had formed a Harrison Club, and old followers of William Henry Harrison's 1840 presidential campaign.

Such occasions were a perfect fit for Harrison. As one of his contemporaries, Depew, noted, Harrison had few equals when it came to public speaking. "He was most lucid and convincing and had what few orators possess," said Depew, "the ability to make a fresh speech every day and a good one. It was a talent of presenting questions from many angles, each of which illuminated his subject and captivated his audience." In his speeches, Harrison often spoke on the Republicans' main issue—maintaining the protective tariff as the best way to promote high wages for American workers by safeguarding U.S. products from foreign competition. "Can we look for contentment if the workingman is only able to supply his daily necessities by his daily toil, but is not able in the vigor of youth

Members of the Tippecanoe Club—voters from Marion County who had cast their ballots for William Henry Harrison—gather on the lawn of the Harrison residence, July 4, 1888.

to lay up a store against old age?" Harrison asked a delegation of 3,000 Clay County coal miners. "A condition of things that compels the laborer to contemplate want, as an indictment of sickness or disability, is the one that tends to social disorder." He also spoke in favor of the party's platform that had come out against the growth of business monopolies, including "all combination of capital, organized in trusts or otherwise, to control arbitrarily the condition of trade among our citizens." Doing so, he believed, would protect workers' interests, as "ordinarily, capital shares the loss of idleness with labor; but under the operation of a trust, in some of its forms, the wageworker alone suffers loss, while idle capital receives dividends from a trust fund."

When the Harrison League of Indianapolis, a group of 300 African American men, paid a call on the evening of June 30, the candidate shared a moving story from his childhood. Harrison recalled that as a boy he had been walking around his grandfather's orchard at North Bend, which stood on the boundary line between Ohio, a free state, and Kentucky, a slave state. While walking Harrison saw in an alder thicket a black man "with the frightened look of a fugitive in his eye. . . . He noticed my approach with a fierce, startled look, to see whether I was likely to betray him; I was frightened myself and left him in some trepidation, but I kept his secret." To shouts of "good!" from the crowd for his actions, Harrison went on to promise that if he became president, he would work to see that their vote counted and they would have a voice in their government.

During Harrison's talks to the various delegations, Tibbott stood by to take notes, which he transcribed and gave to the candidate to review before giving them to the Associated Press for distribution to newspapers across the country. To bolster Harrison's statements on the tariff issue, Republican officials, thanks to heavy financial support from business and industry, were able to blanket the country with pamphlets and handbills touting the protective tariff and lambasting the Democrats for supporting free trade. In Philadelphia alone a group of eleven businessmen subscribed $10,000 each for a "campaign of education" on the tariff question, and the head of a Republican advisory board noted the party had raised $200,000 "so quickly that the Democrats never knew anything about it." Former presidential nominee Blaine provided crucial support, helping to raise money and giving speeches on Harrison's behalf. Blaine received his reward for his efforts after Harrison's eventual victory, being named as secretary of state, the second time he served in that post.

The initial skepticism of Harrison's friends and Republican leaders about his speeches gave way to admiration. "I want to tell you how much you have gained by your meaty speeches—without making a mistake," Congressman John A. Anderson, a college friend, wrote Harrison. "You don't know how rapidly you are growing in public esteem for common sense and great

The spirit of our men is up,
From Rocky hills to Ocean.

CUMBERLAND, M'

IN '88, AS THEY DID THEN,
We roll it now for gallant BEN.

people will, at next election.
Protection

intellectual ability." Matthew Quay, chairman of the Republican National Committee, said of Harrison's "wonderful speeches" that if the candidate had the strength to continue making them until the end of the campaign, "we could safely close these headquarters and he could elect himself."

Michener marveled at his candidate's campaign skills, calling Harrison "a superb strategist and tactician in political warfare," and especially able "in the details of organization and the selection of methods." The grind of giving so many impromptu talks did wear on Harrison. "Even at home, when I sit down at the table with my family," he joked, "I have some apprehensions lest someone may propose a toast and insist that I shall respond."

In addition to the publicity generated by Harrison's speeches in Indianapolis, his efforts to reach the White House were aided by a friend

Opposite and Above: D. E. Brocket of Cumberland, Maryland, designed and built this steel-rigged and canvas-covered campaign ball to promote Harrison's 1888 campaign, taking it 5,000 miles to the candidate's Indianapolis home. The ball was a replica of one built for William Henry Harrison's 1840 campaign.

A poster promoting the 1888 Republican ticket and tying it to the log-cabin campaign of William Henry Harrison.

and fellow Civil War veteran—Lew Wallace. At Harrison's urging, Wallace produced a brief campaign biography to introduce the candidate to those who knew little about him. "I see by the papers that Genl. Wallace is to biograph you," a friend from Colorado wrote Harrison. "That is excellent. He did so well on *Ben-Hur* that we can trust him with Ben Him." Given only a month to do the work, Wallace moved to Indianapolis from his home in Crawfordsville to listen to Harrison's speeches and obtain information from his subject. The author had a free hand in writing the book, as, he noted, Harrison "neither read nor heard read one line of the text." Averaging writing thirty-four pages a day, Wallace was able to meet his deadline, and the book was published on September 1. In the book's preface Wallace apologized that, due to his tight deadline, the book contained "many crudities in the way of unstudied sentences and inappropriate paragraphing, not to speak of words badly chosen." It nonetheless did what it was intended to do— promote Harrison to a wide audience. For many years afterward, Wallace's work remained as the best and most authoritative biography of the Hoosier politician.

Newspapermen worked overtime to get the inside scoop on the "real" Harrison, interviewing the candidate's neighbors and shop owners with whom he had done business. Reporters learned Harrison's hat size (seven and a half, the largest in the state), his favorite shoe (a "square-tipped English four lace Balmoral gaiter," priced at ten dollars), and that he bought from a local tobacconist Havana cigars by the hundreds. An employee at the L.S. Ayres and Company department store confided to a reporter from the *Chicago Tribune* about Harrison's thriftiness when it came to buying suits, saying the candidate never paid less than forty-five dollars nor more than fifty-five dollars, and that the coat he wore on the day he was nominated was one made for him three years ago.

Both parties made use of Harrison's choice of hats—a high hat made of felted beaver fur. Cartoonists for newspapers supporting the Democratic Party often lampooned Harrison by drawing him in a hat far too big for his short stature, and Cleveland adherents took to singing at rallies, "His Grandfather's Hat—It's Too Big for Ben." For their part, Republicans responded with their own campaign song that said:

> Yes: Grandfather's hat fits Ben—fits Ben.
> He wears it with dignified grace,
> > Oh, yes!
> So rally again and we'll put Uncle Ben
> Right back in his grandfather's place.

Although at the beginning of the campaign Harrison had called for the two parties to "encamp upon the high plains of principle and not in the low swamps of personal defamation or detraction," his hopes were dashed by the 1888 election's two great controversies—one that damaged Cleveland's chances, and one that hurt Harrison. The first broadside came in October with what became known as the Murchison Letter. A California Republican had sent a letter, signed as Charles F. Murchison, to Sir Lionel Sackville-West, the British minister (ambassador) to the United States, asking his advice on how to vote. Not suspecting a trap, Sackville-West answered the letter with friendly words and support for the Cleveland administration as the best choice for British interests in spite of recent tensions over a dispute regarding fishing rights in Canada. Republican officials released Sackville-West's letter to the press. The seemingly friendly relations between the hated British and the Cleveland administration infuriated Irish-American voters in New York, and Cleveland had to call for Sackville-West to be dismissed.

Shortly after the Murchison Letter had caused such a furor, the Democrats struck political gold with another letter, this one involving

"Not as heavy as Grover, perhaps, but then I have more lemons."

An editorial cartoon lampoons Harrison using a "campaign lemon squeezer" to squeeze donations from political appointees for his 1888 presidential effort. The caption reads: "Not as heavy as Grover, perhaps, but then I have more lemons."

William W. Dudley served in the Civil War with the Nineteenth Indiana Volunteer Infantry Regiment, losing his right leg during the Battle of Gettysburg. After the war he became commissioner of pensions in both the James Garfield and Chester Arthur administrations.

William W. Dudley, the Republican National Committee treasurer, and featured the class of voter known as a "floater," a person with no fixed party allegiance who sold his ballot to the highest bidder, be it Republican or Democrat. Party workers could buy these votes for as little as two dollars or as high as twenty dollars in close elections and, since political parties, not the state, printed and furnished ballots to voters, could ensure that once a "floater" was bought, he stayed bought. "This infamous practice," complained the *Shelbyville Republican*, "kept up year after year by both parties, has brought about a state of affairs that cannot be contemplated without a shudder." The newspaper went on to lament that a third of the state's voting population "can be directly influenced by the use of money on the day of election."

In a letter sent to an Indiana Republican county chairman, Dudley warned that "only boodle and fraudulent votes and false counting of returns can beat us in the State [Indiana]." To counter this threat, he advised Republican workers to find out what Democrats at the polls were responsible for bribing voters and steer committed Democratic supporters to them, thereby exhausting the opposition's cash stockpile. The most damaging part of the letter, however, appeared in a sentence where Dudley advised: "Divide the voters into blocks of five, and put a trusted man, with necessary funds, in charge of these five, and make them responsible that none get away."

The political dynamite in Dudley's letter found its way to the opposition thanks to a Democratic mail clerk on the Ohio and Mississippi Railroad who was suspicious about the large amount of mail being passed from Republican headquarters to Indiana Republicans. He opened one of the letters, recognized its value to his party, and passed the damaging contents to the Indiana Democratic State Central Committee. The *Sentinel* printed the letter on October 31, 1888, under a banner headline reading: "The Plot

November 17, 1888, cover for Frank Leslie's Illustrated Newspaper *depicts the celebration at Harrison's Indianapolis home following his election as president.*

to Buy Indiana." Although an indignant Dudley and other top Republican officials declared that the letter was a forgery, and denounced the person responsible for interfering with the mail, its contents received nationwide attention, with newspapers supporting the Democratic cause, including the *Sentinel*, happy to lambast Harrison for his ties to such chicanery, while Republican papers defended their candidate's character. Michener, a political veteran, said that the instructions Dudley outlined were standard practice by both parties in Indiana, and found nothing in the letter "unusual, illegal or immoral."

What effect both scandals had on the campaign's outcome is still debated by historians, with Charles Calhoun, in his book on the 1888 election, arguing that underhanded practices by both parties in New York and Indiana "may well have canceled each other out." Whatever the impact nationally, in Indiana the Dudley letter had failed to dampen the enthusiasm of Hoosier Republicans for their favorite son. The day before the election, Harrison, on his way to his downtown law office, was greeted with applause and cheering. On Election Day, Tuesday, November 6, Harrison walked from his home, accompanied by his son, Russell, to Coburn's Livery Stable at Seventh Street between Delaware and Alabama Streets, the polling place for the third precinct of the second ward. To a cry from a supporter of "There comes the next President," Harrison cast the ballot he had carried with him from his house.

After voting, Harrison returned home to learn his fate as a candidate, with regular reports coming to him in his library through a special telegraph wire connecting him with Republican headquarters in New York. After the polls closed, downtown streets in Indianapolis were clogged with people eager to hear the results, with many gathering near newspaper offices to receive reports. "As the morning drew nearer," noted an article in the *Indianapolis Journal*, "the wild crowd, growing hilarious with excitement, would receive a return with cheers, and the next moment follow it up with a refrain of 'Bye, Grover, bye; O, good-bye, old Grover, good-bye.' Another return, and 'What's the matter with Harrison? He's all right.''

A number of people gathered around a large, oval writing table in Harrison's library to consult the returns. When vote totals arrived over the wire from New York, they were read aloud, sometimes by Harrison and sometimes by his law partners, while Russell sorted bulletins by state. The *Journal* described the scene as "a quiet gathering of a few neighbors," adding that Harrison seemed "cool and self-possessed," sometimes retreating to the parlor to talk with his wife, Caroline, and her guests. According to one account, when returns from the state of New York seemed discouraging, Harrison took the news well, telling his friends to cheer up: "This is no life and death affair. I am very happy here in Indianapolis and will continue to be if I'm not elected. Home is a pretty good place."

Harrison seemed much more concerned about whether he won Indiana, closely perusing returns from each of the state's ninety-two counties. When his son-in-law, at about 11:00 p.m., announced that it looked as if Indiana had been won, Harrison responded: "That's enough for me tonight then. My own State is for me. I'm going to bed." Asked the next morning how he could go to sleep still not knowing whether he had won the presidency, Harrison noted that his staying up would not have changed the results if he had lost, and if he won he knew he "had a hard day ahead of me. So I thought a night's rest was best in any event."

Harrison won the presidency, securing the Electoral College with 233 votes to 168 for Cleveland. Harrison had been able to grab the crucial states of New York and Indiana, winning both by the barest of margins (by 2,376 votes in the Hoosier State and 14,373 votes in New York; in both states turnout exceeded 90 percent); both of these were states that Cleveland had captured in the 1884 election. In the popular vote, Cleveland bested Harrison, with 5,534,488 votes to 5,443,892 for his opponent, becoming the third of five presidential candidates to win the popular vote but lose in the Electoral College. The other losing candidates were Andrew Jackson in 1824, Samuel Tilden in 1876, Al Gore in 2000, and Hillary Clinton in 2016.

Cleveland seemed upbeat in spite of his defeat, telling a friend it was "better to be defeated battling for an honest principle than to win by cowardly subterfuge. . . . We were defeated, it is true, but the principles of tariff reform will surely win in the end." The defeated president's wife, Frances, seemed confident that she and her husband would be back, telling a White House servant, upon leaving Washington, D.C., after Harrison's inaguration, "I want you to take good care of all the furniture and ornaments in the house, for I want to find everything just as it is now when we come back again. We are coming back, just four years from today."

Cleveland's supporters blamed bribery for costing their candidate victory in New York and Indiana. Left unsaid, as Calhoun pointed out in his history of the election, was the violent suppression of African American voters in the South by Democrats: Cleveland swept all of the former slave states. Democratic national chairman Calvin S. Brice congratulated Harrison on making a great race and "winning the greatest prize on this earth. I do not mean the Presidency merely but the Presidency—worthy to have it and worthily won." The *Sentinel* admitted after the election that the pro-Republican results (the party had won the White House and both houses of Congress) had to "be accepted as a popular verdict against tariff reform and in favor of the extreme protective policy advocated by the Chicago [Republican] platform."

Brice was not the only one to offer his congratulations on a race well run. At his home in Indianapolis Harrison had to contend with a crush of laudatory letters and telegrams from friends and strangers alike. He also was besieged by those who supported his election expecting to be rewarded with jobs in his new administration. An overwhelmed Harrison wrote his cousin: "I am worked to the verge of despair in receiving callers and trying by the aid of two stenographers and typewriters to deal with my mail. One person could not open and read the letters that come to me. I have been compelled to put them up in bales and to allow most of the ordinary letters of congratulations to go unanswered." Harrison found that the crushing workload did not subside as he assumed his new duties as the nation's twenty-third president.

6

Mr. President

Since he arrived in Washington, D.C., in 1882, as the *Cleveland Leader*'s national correspondent, journalist Frank G. Carpenter had reported on the comings and goings of politicians in his regular column, "Carp's Washington." The nation's capital was a city "like no other in the world," he said, "a living curiosity, made up of the strangest and most incongruous elements."

Although used to Washington's quirks, Carpenter was still taken aback in the spring of 1888 when he spied the country's new president—Benjamin Harrison—in a time before the U.S. Secret Service protected the chief executive, taking long walks on Connecticut Avenue clad in a plain black overcoat and wearing a pair of brown kid gloves, a tall hat, and a shining black silk tie. "President Harrison, in his daily habits," reported Carpenter, "is showing himself more democratic than any of his predecessors of the past decade. He sees no reason why his change of address from Indianapolis to Washington should limit his moving about as freely as in the past."

Since his inauguration on March 4, 1889, Harrison had been seen regularly walking on the city's busiest streets, exercise deemed necessary, perhaps, because his belly had been growing over the years. "I have seen him enter a store to make a purchase just like any shopper," Carpenter wrote, "and he has been known to drink a glass of soda water here, as he used to in the drugstore back home." The reporter pointed out that while

Benjamin Harrison kept closemouthed when it came to news about who would serve in his administration, telling reporters after his election: "I am only a listener *now and for some time to come."*

Harrison was reputed to be "cold and indifferent" in his dealings with even high officials of his own Republican Party, much less with strangers, Carpenter had found him to be "genial and pleasant, cordial and free in expressing his opinions, but decided in his refusal to allow me to publish them."

Further describing Harrison as "a meticulous man," Carpenter added that during his first weeks in the White House the new president had endured constant interruptions from a stream of well-wishers and those seeking jobs in his new administration. To the reporter, it seemed as if Harrison did not possess former president Chester A. Arthur's "facility of unloading minor responsibilities upon the shoulders of his helpers." Harrison himself later reflected of the early days of his time in the White House that it was a "rare piece of good fortune" if he was able to have "one wholly uninterrupted hour" at his desk per day. "His [the president's] time is so broken into bits that he is often driven to late night work," said Harrison, "or to set up a desk in his bedroom when preparing a message or other paper requiring unbroken attention." There were even times when Harrison, harried by office seekers, felt "like a hunted animal," surrounded by people always wanting something from him. His view is not surprising, considering that his White House office had to contend with, on average, seven hundred letters each day. Harrison had to hire extra clerks to handle Sunday mail so that his regular office staff could have the day off for religious services.

Carpenter had hit on something that typified Harrison's four years in the White House—his tendency to be a hands-on, active chief executive when it came to determining and acting on his administration's policies. He worked closely with the Republican-controlled Fifty-First Congress from 1891 to 1893, a period in which six states were added to the Union (North Dakota, South Dakota, Montana, Washington, Idaho, and Wyoming) and appropriations grew so fast that Democrats complained about a "billion-dollar Congress." The powerful Speaker of the House Thomas B. Reed had a terse response to any complaints from his opponents: "This is a billion-dollar country."

Before the 1892 midterm election swept away its majority in the House of Representatives, the Republican Congress shepherded passage of 531 public laws, including such major legislation as higher tariffs (the

The Harrisons stop to greet a crowd at Bridgeport, Pennsylvania, on their way to take up residence at the White House in Washington, D.C., February 26, 1889.

Above: *Chief Justice of the Supreme Court Melville W. Fuller administers the oath of office to Harrison on the east portico of the U.S. Capitol, March 4, 1889.* *Opposite:* *First-page draft of Harrison's inaugural address.*

McKinley Tariff Act), protection of trade and commerce from monopolies (the Sherman Anti-Trust Act), increased pensions for invalid veterans and their dependents (Dependent Pension Act), and authority for the president to set aside forest reserves from land in the public domain (the Forest Reserve Act). "No Congress in peace time since the first has passed so many great & important measures of lasting value to the people," said Republican congressman Henry Cabot Lodge.

Harrison had set out the goals for his administration for all Americans to hear in his inaugural address, delivered in a heavy rain that drenched

~~Fellow Citizens~~ ~~Citizens~~ the constitution there is no
constitutional or legal requirement that
the President ~~shall~~ take the oath of office
in the presence of the people. The demands
of the law would be fully satisfied by
a private administration of the oath
by a competent officer. But there is
so manifest an
~~an~~ appropriateness in the ~~accustomed~~ public
induction of the Chief Executive officer
of the Nation into his great office that from
the beginning of the ~~other~~ government the people
to whom service the official oath conveyed
the officer have been ~~admitted~~ ~~called to~~
witness the solemn ceremonial, the oath taken in
the presence of the ~~vast gathering of~~ the
people becomes a Covenant — the officer
covenanting to serve the whole body of the
people here ~~represented~~ by a faithful
and fearless execution of the laws — of
all the laws — ~~everywhere~~ ~~wherever~~ these
~~everywhere~~, so that they may be the unfailing
defense and security of those who respect
and observe them, and that ~~no~~ ~~under that~~
~~Shield of~~ ~~reverence~~ neither wealth, station or

V 69   1

those attending the ceremonies on the terrace at the east front of the Capitol. With memories of his grandfather, William Henry Harrison, taking sick and dying after delivering his long-winded inaugural speech forty-eight years earlier, perhaps still in his mind, Benjamin Harrison took the precaution of wearing chamois-skin underwear for protection against the inclement weather. In his approximately 4,000-word speech, he compared the America of yesteryear with that of the present—"thirty-eight populous and prosperous States . . . [and] thirteen States, weak in everything except courage and the love of liberty."

The new president also touched upon the need for a continued protective tariff so American industry could thrive, possibly changing immigration laws "as to make the inquiry into the character and good disposition of persons applying for citizenship more careful and searching," the need for a modern navy, increased pensions for Union veterans and their widows and orphans, and that the people of all congressional districts had an interest in ensuring elections in each "shall truly express the views and wishes of a majority of the qualified electors residing within it." Harrison called for easing of tensions between the two political parties, with each respecting the others' opinions. He ended his address by seeing a hopeful future, noting:

> I do not mistrust the future. Dangers have been in frequent ambush along our path, but we have uncovered and vanquished them all. Passion has swept some of our communities, but only to give us a new demonstration that the great body of our people are stable, patriotic, and law-abiding. No political party can long pursue advantage at the expense of public honor or by rude and indecent methods without protest and fatal disaffection in its own body. The peaceful agencies of commerce are more fully revealing the necessary unity of all our communities, and the increasing intercourse of our people is promoting mutual respect. We shall find unalloyed pleasure in the

revelation which our next census will make of the swift development of the great resources of some of the States. Each State will bring its generous contribution to the great aggregate of the nation's increase. And when the harvests from the fields, the cattle from the hills, and the ores of the earth shall have been weighed, counted, and valued, we will turn from them all to crown with the highest honor the State that has most promoted education, virtue, justice, and patriotism among its people.

Inaugural parade for Harrison makes it way down Pennsylvania Avenue.

From the start of his administration, Harrison stood steadfast against key party leaders, including Thomas C. Platt of New York and Matthew Quay of Pennsylvania, in making sure that qualified individuals—not just party stooges—received appointments to key government positions, earning a reputation as the "White House iceberg." Platt observed that outside of his official duties, Harrison could be "a courtly gentleman," but when evaluating those who sought official appointments "he was as glacial as a Siberian stripped of his furs. During and after an interview, if one could secure it, one felt even in torrid weather like pulling on his winter flannels, galoshes, overcoat, mitts and earlaps." Even Reed fell out with the president, with the Speaker of the House noting that he had only two enemies in his life, and Harrison had pardoned one from a

Harrison's private secretary, Elijah W. Halford, at work at his desk.

prison sentence and had given the other man a patronage job as collector for the Port of Portland in Maine. And although the president offended men such as Platt and Quay who expected government jobs for their party favorites, Harrison won no plaudits from civil service reformers, who believed his efforts did not go far enough. (Harrison did give future president Theodore Roosevelt his first national office, as a civil service commissioner.)

Elijah W. Halford, a former newspaperman with the *Indianapolis Journal* who served as Harrison's private secretary, recalled that when his boss took office, he was still an "unknown quantity to many fancied 'leaders,' particularly with some who subsequently felt themselves called to be the appointed guardians or administrators of one who could scarcely be trusted to walk in Presidential ways without their aid." With that kind of attitude, he added, it was no wonder that "no small degree of friction . . . developed" between the president and party leaders.

Halford remembered a time when Quay, the Republican Party's national chairman and a senator from Pennsylvania, came calling to secure positions for a list of names supported by himself and his fellow senator from Pennsylvania. Although Quay vouched for the men under consideration, Harrison balked, insisting on making his own inquiries into their fitness for the positions. Halford quoted the president as telling Quay that he "could not consent to the surrender of the personal responsibility for appointments which the Constitution enjoined, and he would have proper inquiries initiated on his own behalf, and he hoped the result would be to corroborate the judgment of the senators." Harrison also stood firm against a request from Secretary of State James G. Blaine, who had wanted his son, Walker, to receive a position as first assistant secretary of state. Although the president did approve giving Walker another job in the department, the incident, noted Halford, "resulted in a rankling that never healed."

Harrison's White House office before the building underwent electrification.

Taking up his duties as the nation's chief executive from an office next to the Cabinet Room, the same space used as an office by President Abraham Lincoln, Harrison, unlike today's presidents, had only a small staff to assist him. The staff included a private secretary (Halford, nicknamed "Lige" and "Brother Halford" by the president) and an assistant secretary, along with stenographers, a telegraph operator, and doorkeepers. One

Harrison and his cabinet, 1893. Left to right: Stephen B. Elkins, Secretary of War; John W. Noble, Secretary of the Interior; John W. Foster, Secretary of State; John Wanamaker, Postmaster General; Harrison; Benjamin F. Tracy, Secretary of the Navy; Charles Foster, Secretary of the Treasury; Jeremiah M. Rusk, Secretary of the Agriculture; and William H. H. Miller, Attorney General.

longtime worker at the White House remembered that everyone employed there "knew everyone else and there was a feeling of 'all one family' impossible in later years," even though Harrison was viewed as "aloof and reserved a man as ever filled the office, though not so cold as his exterior suggested." Harrison's reserve might be explained by how he viewed the burdens of his office. Returning one afternoon after a walk with Halford, the president pointed to the White House and observed, "There is my jail."

Harrison started his day with breakfast at about 8:00 a.m. followed by religious devotions and prayer. The president usually met with callers in his office from 9:30 a.m. or 10:00 a.m. until 1:00 p.m., with congressmen invited to call on him between 11:00 a.m. and 12:30 p.m. Tuesday through Friday. Lunch was at 1:30 p.m. and his family dinner occurred at 6:30 p.m. Meetings with members of his cabinet were held twice weekly, and Harrison also met with individual cabinet officials on a weekly basis. When needed, he hosted dinner parties to discuss strategy with Republicans in Congress on major legislation, called "Ben Harrison's Silver Dinners," and also gave numerous speeches throughout the country touting his administration's goals and achievements. For example, he embarked on a speaking tour in the Midwest covering 3,000 miles in which he gave more than forty speeches, and a subsequent Southern and Pacific Coast jaunt of more than 9,000 miles in which Harrison gave 140 impromptu speeches.

If administration officials took sick and could not fulfill their duties, Harrison took on their work. At one point Halford observed that the president had "practically the details of four Departments to look over" due to illnesses. One top administration official noted that if he wanted to find out anything about the government he went to the president, as he "knew more than anyone else." John J. Ingalls, a senator from Kansas, believed that Harrison, up to that time, had been the only man who served as president capable of "discharging with signal ability the duty of every one of his cabinet ministers; that he was the best equipped man that had ever been in public life." This view was echoed by Harrison's friend and political confidant Louis T. Michener, who noted that every member of the president's cabinet told him repeatedly Harrison knew more about what was going on in every department of government than did their various heads, and "they never went to him to discuss departmental matters with him without coming away filled with amazement, because of his wonderful knowledge, as well as the unerring accuracy of his mental operation."

Four generations in the Harrison White House, left to right: Caroline Scott Harrison, Benjamin Harrison McKee ("Baby McKee), Mary Harrison, Mary Lodge McKee, and John W. Scott.

Russell Harrison (left) on the White House lawn holding the hand of his daughter, Marthena, while pet dog Jack sits at their feet. In the goat cart drawn by Old Whiskers are Russell's nephew, Benjamin (Baby McKee), and his niece, Mary Lodge McKee.

The added workload sometimes took its toll on Harrison, with Halford able to gauge the president's mood by the morning greeting he received: "When I see him in the morning and he greets me with, 'Halford, how are you today?' I sit down by his desk for a pleasant talk about matters. When he greets me with, 'Good morning, Mr. Halford.' I bolt the door and wait until after lunch for the talk."

In addition to his habit of taking on too much work for himself, Harrison's mood might have been affected by the overcrowding he and his family had to deal with in their new living quarters. It was a full house. Harrison and his wife, Caroline, were joined by their daughter,

Mary McKee, her two children—Benjamin Harrison McKee (called Baby McKee by the press, who loved writing stories about the child) and Mary Lodge McKee. Mary's husband, Robert, also visited, as well as Harrison's son, Russell, whose wife and daughter lived in the White House while he attended to business.

Caroline eventually invited her elderly father, John W. Scott, to live in the White House, and her niece, Mary Scott Lord "Mame" Dimmick, frequently visited and helped her aunt with her social obligations and her correspondence as First Lady and often accompanied Harrison on his walks. All these people had to jostle for rooms in a building equipped with limited living space for a large family. "Very few people understand to what straits the President's family has been put at times for lack of accommodations," Caroline told a reporter. "Really there are only five sleeping apartments and there is no feeling of privacy."

Left: A smiling Harrison poses with his grandson, Baby McKee. *Right:* Caroline Scott Harrison in the dress she wore for her husband's inauguration.

The First Lady hit upon a bold plan to update the ninety-year-old
White House (then known as the Executive Mansion), whose first
occupant had been President John Adams. Renovations had been made
to the building during the administration of Chester A. Arthur, but much

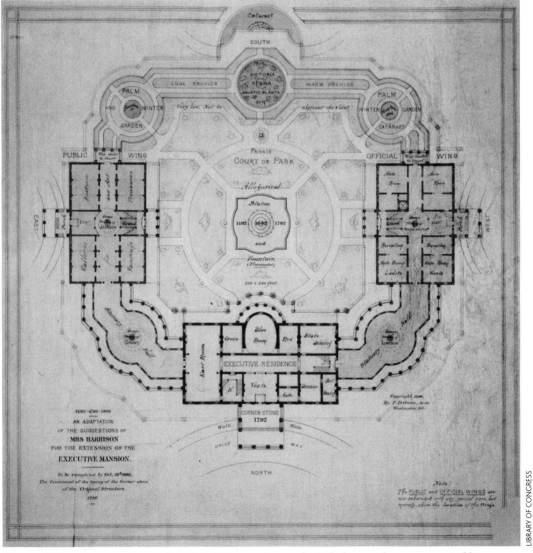

*Proposed plans for extensions to the White House and grounds, including garden, as suggested by
Caroline Scott Harrison.*

work still needed to be done, with many in Washington referring to the White House as "a moldy old mansion." Caroline confided in her diary that "rats have nearly taken the building so it has become necessary to get a man with ferrets" to confront the problem. The U.S. Army Corps of Engineers had suggested building an executive office building to the west of the White House, while some had even called for constructing a new building to house the president elsewhere in Washington, D.C. "We are here four years," said Caroline. "I do not look beyond that, as many things occur in that time, but I am anxious to see the family of the President provided for properly, and while I am here I hope to get the present building into good condition."

Caroline worked with architect Frederick D. Owen to come up with plans for adding wings to both sides of the White House, titled "Mrs. Harrison's Suggestion for the Extension of the Executive Mansion." A new West Wing would be devoted to offices and a new East Wing to an art gallery, leaving the existing mansion for a residence and for entertaining. A conservatory was planned for the southern end of the grounds as well as a fountain commemorating Christopher Columbus's "discovery" of America. This extensive renovation would be, she suggested, an appropriate way to commemorate the centennial celebration of George Washington's inauguration as the country's first president.

Harrison himself saw the need for changes to the mansion. He later noted that the White House stood as "an office and home combined—an evil combination. There is no break in the day—no change of atmosphere. The blacksmith, when the allotted hours of work are over, banks his fire, lays aside his leather apron, washes his grimy hands and goes home. And he gets a taste of unsmoked morning air before he resumes his work." Also, everyone else in public service enjoyed having "an unroofed space between the bedroom and the desk." The president, however, had only a door that

Telegraph office, White House.

always remained unlocked between his office and "what was not very accurately called his private apartments," Harrison noted.

Unfortunately, Caroline's plans failed to pass legislative scrutiny, falling victim to a patronage dispute between her husband and Reed. Congress did appropriate $35,000 to renovate the mansion, and Caroline set out to do all she could to make it habitable, as well as preparing an inventory of its contents, finding such items as a gold-boarded mirror that came from Paris during President James Monroe's administration. Improvement projects included installation of private bathrooms with all the bedrooms, new wallpaper and paint, a new kitchen, improving the rotting floors, acquiring new furnishings, adding greenhouses, and overall improvements to public

White House upstairs corridor.

areas. The new bathrooms particularly impressed the president. "The greatest beauty of all is the work in the bathroom—with the white tile and marble and porcelain-lined tub," Harrison told his wife. "They would tempt a duck to wash himself every day."

The Harrisons seemed to never let their exalted positions go to their heads. Halford remembered that on afternoons when he needed the president's signature on a document, or to relay vital information, he found his boss sitting at the window of his sitting room reading. "Opposite him would be Mrs. Harrison engaged in decorating china," said Halford. "Often he would be reading aloud to her while she kept on with her painting. The White House did not change the family life of their Indiana home." Caroline reintroduced dancing to the White House and put up the first decorated Christmas tree in the mansion.

A major change to the mansion came with the addition of electric lights and call bells, overseen by civilian electricians from the Edison Company, including Irwin "Ike" Hoover, later longtime chief usher at the White House. Hoover took over as the permanent electrician at the mansion, and discovered that the Harrisons, with whom he had talked to at length, were wary of the new system. "Electricity in practice was an unknown and fearsome quantity to the lay mind," he recalled, "and I found the family and servants afraid to touch the lights." Hoover soon made it a practice to turn the lights on in the halls and parlors in the evening, and turn them off when he returned in the morning. "All were fascinated by this new thing, even if fearing it, and asked endless questions," Hoover recalled.

The White House renovation also gave Caroline the opportunity to promote a cause she believed in: fine arts. For many years she had been interested in painting, including china and porcelain painting, which she had learned from an Indianapolis-based artist named Paul Putzki, who later taught classes in the art at the White House. She also took watercolor painting lessons from an artist named J. Henry Moser. "I have had a great many talented pupils, but none with more enthusiasm and genuine love for the art," Moser said of Caroline. "She devotes her time to it, not because it is a fad for women to paint nowadays, nor for any desire to distinguish herself, but purely for the enjoyment of painting and the happiness it gives her immediate family." She also used her skills to decorate porcelain dishes to give as souvenirs, and was responsible for the beginnings of the famous White House china collection.

Being in the public gaze was not all positive for the First Lady. Caroline became entangled in a controversy that received nationwide newspaper attention. It involved a gift to her in July 1890 by Postmaster General

John Wanamaker and some of his friends of a vacation cottage located on Cape May Point in New Jersey, a perfect place to escape Washington, D.C.'s oppressive summer heat.

Although Harrison had sent a $10,000 check to Wanamaker for the twenty-room cottage, opposition newspapers questioned the transaction, with the *New York Sun* asking in an editorial: "Who are these generous individuals that have bestowed upon MRS. BENJAMIN HARRISON a cottage at Cape May Point, clear of encumbrance and with floors swept clean for BABY MC KEE to creep over this summer?" The newspaper demanded that the names of those involved in the gift be made public, as the president "who takes a bribe is a lost President." A distraught Caroline confided to a White House staffer, "What have we ever done that we should be held up to ridicule by newspapers, and the President be so cruelly attacked, and even his little helpless grandchildren be made fun of, for the country to laugh at!" If such public scorn was the price paid for being president, she wished that the "Good Lord will deliver my husband from any future experience."

As they do it seems with nearly every president, legislative failures and controversies plagued the administration. Although Republicans in Congress had enjoyed success early in Harrison's presidency, they failed in one major endeavor—an attempt to safeguard African American voting rights in the South, an issue Harrison had addressed during the 1888 campaign and in his inaugural, and a natural move for a party needing black votes to have any chance of success in the South. With Democrats in southern states striving to disenfranchise black voters by every means necessary, including intimidation and violence, Harrison had asked in his first annual message to Congress:

> When and under what conditions is the black man to have a free ballot?
> When is he in fact to have those full civil rights which have so long
> been his in law? When is that equality of influence which our form of

government was intended to secure to the electors to be restored? This generation should courageously face these grave questions, and not leave them as a heritage of woe to the next. The consultation should proceed with candor, calmness, and great patience, upon the lines of justice and humanity, not of prejudice and cruelty. No question in our country can be at rest except upon the firm base of justice and of the law.

Massachusetts congressman Lodge helped put different proposals into legislation to ensure that African American voters would receive equal treatment at the ballot box. His Federal Election Bill placed congressional races under the supervision of the federal government, a measure that squeaked by in the House by a vote of 155 to 149. Democratic opponents

Big Foot's camp three weeks after the Wounded Knee Massacre, with bodies of several Lakota Sioux people wrapped in blankets in the foreground and U.S. soldiers in the background.

labeled the legislation a "Force Bill," and made sinister insinuations that federal troops would return to the South to enforce its measures by threat of the bayonet (actually, federal circuit courts would have authority). Other Republican-backed legislation took precedent in the U.S. Senate, delaying the Lodge Bill's consideration. Senate Democrats used every legislative trick they could to ensure the matter never came to a vote, helped, in great part, by Vice President Levi Morton's impartiality as presiding officer, much to the chagrin of fellow Republicans, as well as assistance from Western senators seeking support for increases in silver purchases by the federal government. "That the majority shall rule is an underlying principle of our institutions," a disappointed Harrison said in an interview. "It will not do for the people of any section to say that they must be let alone, that it is a local question to be settled by the States whether we shall have honest elections or not." The Federal Election Bill marked the last gasp of civil rights legislation for African Americans well into the next century, as racial segregation laws continued to expand in the former Confederacy in the Jim Crow era.

Harrison's reputation in regard to Native American policy proved to be more problematic. The administration had to contend with news of the massacre by soldiers from the U.S. Army's Seventh Cavalry of Lakota Sioux men, women, and children near Wounded Knee Creek on the Lakota Pine Ridge Indian Reservation in South Dakota on December 29, 1890. Harrison's policy on relations with the tribes remaining in the West closely followed that of previous presidents, seeking to "civilize" Native Americans by taking them away from their usual lifestyle, turning them into farmers, and educating them "for the intelligent exercise of his new citizenship," noted Harrison. Seeing their way of life disappearing and their hunting grounds taken by white settlers and being trapped on government reservations, Native Americans desperately turned to a spiritual movement that promised a return to past greatness by performing a ritualistic "ghost dance."

As the Ghost Dance movement spread, whites in the area feared bloodshed. Matters were not helped by the actions of an incompetent government agent dealing with the Pine Ridge Reservation, who sent panicked messages to his superiors in Washington, D.C. Harrison called upon his commissioner of Indian affairs, Thomas J. Morgan, to investigate the situation. Although Morgan offered a compassionate view of the Native Americans, saying they had a right to "expect sympathy, help, and last but by no means least, justice," tragedy ensued at Wounded Knee. While the Seventh Cavalry attempted to disarm the Indians, someone fired a shot, and in the resulting panic, more than a hundred Lakota men, women, and children were killed; twenty-five soldiers were also killed, probably by friendly fire. Although the massacre did not harm the Harrison administration with the public at the time, its memory served as a rallying point for Native American activists in the 1970s and to this day.

Harrison could not have know how much work he would have to do in dealing with one aspect of his administration—foreign affairs. After all, his secretary of state, Blaine, had been in the post in the James Garfield administration, and could presumably be counted upon to efficiently handle his department. Harrison supported Blaine in his department's effort to improve trade relations and establish trade agreements with Latin American countries early in his administration.

Ill health kept Blaine away from his duties for months at a time, with Harrison having to deal with such issues as a dispute among America, England, and Germany about ownership of the Samoan Islands; disagreements with Great Britain about the fur-seal industry in the Bering Sea (Harrison's determination had frustrated a British diplomat enough to have him refer to him as "that obstinate and pugnacious little President");

and a quarrel with Chile after an incident with American sailors from the USS *Baltimore* in a barroom fight with Chileans in Valparaiso, Chile. The *Baltimore* incident, and the resulting messages back and forth between U.S. and Chilean officials, were serious enough to bring the two countries to the brink of war. Harrison deftly and firmly handled the diplomatic crisis and Chilean officials bowed to the president's demands. Even as his time in office wound down, Harrison busied himself in an ultimately failed attempt to annex the Hawaiian Islands for the United States.

At first, relations between Harrison and Blaine had been good, but as time went on the two men seemed to grow apart as the president had to take on more and more responsibility for foreign affairs due to Blaine's absences. Diplomat John W. Foster, who served as a sort of middleman between Harrison and Blaine, and later took over as secretary of state, noted that during the greater part of his time in office, Blaine was in "poor health, and often was confined to his bed or room for weeks with attacks of sickness." Even Caroline noticed the strain on her husband, and the lack of appreciation he received for his efforts, writing her daughter about Blaine, "I am rather disgusted with the way he [Blaine] & his friends act in the matter. They claim all the credit when your Father has done all the work."

Matters came to head the closer it came to see who would be the Republican nominee for president in 1892. Republican opponents of Harrison still dreamed of Blaine winning the party's nomination at its convention, set to begin on June 7, 1892, in Minneapolis, Minnesota. Other possible contenders for the nomination included Ohio governor and former congressman William McKinley and Harrison's longtime foe Walter Q. Gresham. The president seemed unsure about whether or not to seek another term, writing a friend, "I have not been in any state of eagerness about a re-nomination. The fact is I almost shrink from the labor and worry that is involved in a campaign." He particularly seemed to have no stomach for a prolonged fight, noting that if his renomination "had to be schemed for by me it was, first, pretty clear evidence that it ought not come to me: and, secondly rather a discouraging prospect of success."

As anti-Harrison forces began to gather steam, the president became determined to seek another four years in office, believing he had only two choices—"become a candidate or 'forever wear the name of a political coward.'" He told Michener that nobody in his family had ever "retreated in the presence of a foe without giving battle, and so I have determined to stand and fight." On June 4, a few days before the opening of the Republican convention, Blaine submitted his resignation as secretary of

Harrison (center) relaxes at the summer home of his Secretary of State, James G. Blaine (right, with hat in hand). Standing in the back, left to right, are Henry Cabot Lodge, Walker Blaine, and Halford.

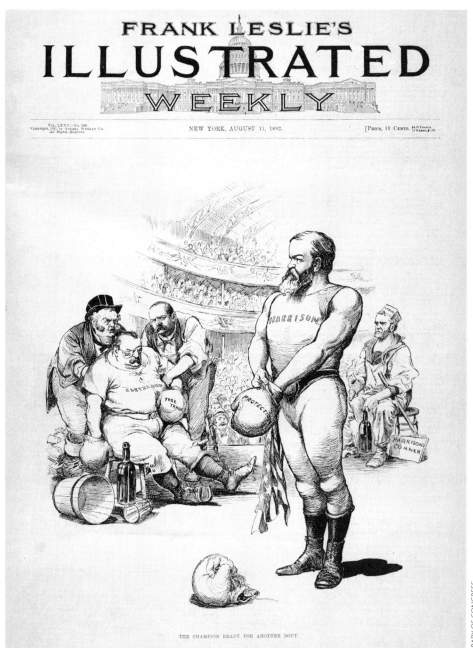

FRANK LESLIE'S
ILLUSTRATED
WEEKLY

VOL. LXXV.—No. 1938.
Copyright, 1892, by AMER'N WEEKLY Co.
All Rights Reserved.

NEW YORK, AUGUST 11, 1892.

[PRICE, 10 CENTS.

THE CHAMPION READY FOR ANOTHER BOUT.

JOHN BULL—" 'Ev another go at him, Grover!"

"*The Champion Ready for Another Bout.*" *Cartoon on the cover of* Frank Leslie's Illustrated Weekly *from August 11, 1892, pictures Harrison ready to again defeat his Democratic opponent, Grover Cleveland, powered by his protectionist policies versus Cleveland's support of free trade.*

state, a move that even one of his friends labeled "the most lamentable act" of his political career.

Speaking to one of his aides about Blaine's resignation, Harrison is supposed to have said: "Well, there is one thing, I am sure to be comfortable for the next 8 or 9 months at any rate." Blaine's supporters pushed his candidacy at the convention, but Harrison prevailed, winning the nomination handily over Blaine and McKinley. Republican insider Mark Hanna, who opposed Harrison's renomination, said that the president's victory "seemed to fall like a wet blanket" upon most of the delegates except for the "ones most interested in his nomination," and predicted "the most lifeless campaign for a half century." The convention abandoned Harrison's previous vice president, Levi Morton, for Whitelaw Reid, a newspaper owner and diplomat. Harrison would be facing a familiar opponent, Grover Cleveland, who the Democrats had nominated for another try at the presidency. Both men also faced a threat from the insurgent Populist Party, which nominated former congressman James Weaver of Iowa as the candidate of its farmer-based interests.

The 1892 presidential contest paled in comparison in every way with the one four years before due to the First Lady's illness. Caroline had been unhappy with her husband's decision to run again, asking him upon hearing the news, "Why, General? Why when it has been so hard for you." Diagnosed with pulmonary tuberculosis, she had vacationed for a time in the Adirondack Mountains in New York to seek some relief from her condition. Caroline's health, however, only worsened, and she returned to the White House in September, cared for by her niece, Mary Dimmick. "Just now I am too full of anxiety about her to think of much else," Harrison wrote a friend. Both candidates refrained from campaigning while the First Lady lay seriously ill. "I so deeply regret Father's inability to help at this time," wrote Harrison's daughter, Mary, "for if he was able to receive some delegations & make some speeches it would be a powerful factor . . . just as it was four years ago."

In addition to his wife's failing health, the president had to deal with serious labor unrest, with strikes by silver miners in Idaho; railroad workers in Buffalo, New York; and steelworkers in Homestead, Pennsylvania, that turned bloody. Harrison had sent troops to quell the strike in Idaho, winning himself no friends among American working men. One midwestern Republican mourned how what once had been "a grand honest people's party" had become "the slave of the money power." For his part, Cleveland pointed to the "tender mercy the workingman receives from those made selfish and sordid by unjust governmental favoritism."

Caroline died on October 25, and the president took his wife to Indianapolis for burial at Crown Hill Cemetery. Harrison's grief at her death

was so great that he failed to return to Indianapolis on November 8 to vote for himself for president. It would not have mattered; Cleveland won solid victories in both the popular vote (5,556,918 to 5,176,108) and the Electoral College (277 to 145); Weaver captured several western states, winning 1,029,846 popular votes and 22 Electoral votes. In addition to winning every state in the South, Cleveland took such critical swing states as New York, New Jersey, Connecticut, and even Harrison's home state, Indiana.

An 1890 portrait of Caroline Scott Harrison.

FRANK LESLIE'S
ILLUS HOMESTEAD TROUBLES. TED
WEEKLY

NEW YORK, JULY 14, 1892.　　[PRICE, 10 CENTS.

THE LABOR TROUBLES AT HOMESTEAD, PENNSYLVANIA—ATTACK OF THE STRIKERS AND THEIR SYMPATHIZERS ON THE SURRENDERED PINKERTON MEN.—DRAWN BY MISS G. A. DAVIS, FROM A SKETCH BY C. UPHAM.—[SEE PAGE 47.]

Cover of the July 14, 1892, issue of Frank Leslie's Illustrated Weekly *depicting the violence of the Homestead strike in Pennsylvania.*

Some Republicans blamed their defeat on workers, the "employee class who secretly and deceitfully votes against their employers from 'pure cussedness.'" Business leaders also took some blame, with Henry Clay Frick, chairman of the Carnegie Steel Company, coming under fire for his stubborn stand against workers in the Homestead strike. The president's effort also suffered from lack of assistance from all party leaders, with some, a reporter told Halford, supportive of Harrison to his face, but acting like Judases when his back was turned.

Harrison felt no sting in his defeat. "Indeed after the heavy blow the death of my wife dealt me," he said, "I do not think I could have stood the strain a re-election would have brought." Harrison confided in a letter to Gilbert A. Pierce, Senator from North Dakota, that the American people were "entitled to their will," and if the programs of the Democratic Party were as wrong and destructive as he believed, the people would find out and "as Mr. [Abraham] Lincoln said 'wobble right.'" The outgoing president added that when he retired from public life after Cleveland took office it would be for life. Harrison wrote:

> I have not enjoyed public life. Indeed it seems to me—measured by my experience and sense of time, without reference to the calendar—that I have been here [in the White House] ten years now. The time has not been broken by any period of relaxation or joyousness. The shadow of great cares have been continually over me. It is a constitutional fault of mine to carry responsibility very heavily.

Harrison, the last Civil War general to serve as chief executive, accompanied Cleveland, the first man to win nonconsecutive terms as president, to his inauguration on March 4, 1893. Members of Harrison's cabinet accompanied him on his way to the train station for his trip home to Indianapolis. His travel time included a stop at Richmond, Indiana, where he addressed a large crowd before a welcoming committee from

PUCK

1889

1893

U.S TREASURY
SURPLUS
$100,000,000.
DOLLARS.

LOOTED

U.S TREAS

"THE PEOPLE WANTED A CHANGE, AND THEY GOT IT."—*Benj. Harrison.*
BUT THE CHANGE WAS MADE IN <u>1889</u>, AND WE ARE STILL SUFFERING FROM IT—PUCK.

A less-than-flattering view of Harrison's time in office from the humor magazine Puck, *accusing him of looting the surplus in the U.S Treasury during his four years in office and leaving Cleveland in a bind.*

Indianapolis met him in nearby Cambridge City. In Indianapolis a cheering throng—as large as the one that had bid him farewell four years before—celebrated his return while a band played "Home, Sweet Home." According to Harrison, crowds jammed Illinois Street, Washington Street, and up Pennsylvania Street to the Denison Hotel. "The reception at the State House in the evening was as great a jam as I ever saw in Indpls—and the cordiality was very touching," Harrison wrote Halford.

Reporting on Harrison's homecoming, the *Indianapolis Journal* noted that no matter a person's political party or religion, "all are proud to have Benjamin Harrison come back to Indiana to live and to be an example of what is true and noble in citizenship." There were some things, the newspaper added, that were better than being president, especially giving the nation "the inspiration of a noble example." Settling in once again in his North Delaware Street residence, accompanied by his daughter, Mary, and his two grandchildren, Harrison wrote his son, Russell, "I made no mistake in coming home at once—there are no friends like the old ones."

Harrison found that those who had been renting his house while he was president had left it in "very fair living condition," and his release from the great cares and responsibilities of being president had made his life easier, he was sleeping well, even after an evening cup of coffee, "and the shake is going out of my pen, so that I can write with comfort." There existed, he admitted to Halford, a sadness involving his homecoming. "If we could have returned an unbroken household," he wrote, referring to the death of Caroline, "my cup of joy would have been full." Unfortunately for Harrison, "there was a cloud over our spirits and sad memories almost obscured the light" from the welcoming smiles of his old neighbors.

7

An Ex-President at Home

Out for his usual stroll near his home on Delaware Street one evening in January 1899, one of Indianapolis's most distinguished citizens found his walk cut short when one of his neighbors ran up to him crying, "Oh! Mr. Harrison, those two men there have robbed my house. They have the plunder in that bag." According to an account published in the *New York Times*, the woman pointed out to the former president two men who were hurrying away from the scene of the crime. The sixty-five-year old Harrison took after them, as best he could, yelling at the criminals to stop, but they continued to flee. Seeing a horse-drawn buggy nearby, he hailed it, told the two men in it what had happened, jumped in, and "gave chase to the flying men," the *Times* reported. "The latter were overtaken and Mr. Harrison jumped out and caught one, but the other escaped."

Not every day of the ex-president's life had such excitement, but Harrison did remain quite busy after leaving the White House and taking up residence again in Indianapolis. "I came back to Indianapolis—for since I came to manhood, I have had no other home," he told a crowd at the Indiana Statehouse upon his return to the city. Although he had received "attractive" offers to move elsewhere, it seemed to him that "the only home for me was Indianapolis." With no presidential pension to draw upon, Harrison returned to his law practice to make his living, restricting

An 1896 portrait of ex-president Benjamin Harrison.

his cases to those with retainers of $500 or more and serving only as an associate to another attorney, sometimes earning fees as high as $25,000 and even arguing, and winning, a case before the U.S. Supreme Court. Stanford University in California paid him $25,000 (a handsome sum in those days) for a series of six lectures on the law and the development of the early U.S. Constitution, an opportunity he used not to make lawyers but to "promote a broad and intelligent American citizenship. Our civil institutions are safe only while in the keeping of a generation that loves them; and the love of institutions—however it may be with another sort—must be educated." Any responsible citizen, he noted, must first have independence of thought. "Individual independence necessarily precedes community independence," Harrison said. "The free man came before the free state; and the free state will not survive him."

In addition to his law practice and lectures, Harrison also wrote articles for national magazines, including the *Ladies' Home Journal*, which paid him $5,000 for nine pieces that later appeared in book form as *This Country of Ours* (1898), and he served on the board of trustees for Purdue University in West Lafayette, Indiana. He turned down two interesting job opportunities, the presidency of a bank and an endowed professorship at the University of Chicago. For relaxation, Harrison vacationed in the Adirondack Mountains at Old Forge, New York, eventually buying a camp he named Berkeley Lodge, the same name as the Virginia plantation of his great-grandfather.

Although a financial panic gripped the nation in 1893, and bedeviled the Grover Cleveland administration, Harrison prospered. He also continued to be involved in politics, using a skill at which he always excelled, delivering speeches promoting the Republican Party and its policies as the best way forward for the country. His views offered a notable contrast to Democrat William Jennings Bryan's call for the free coinage of silver and abandoning the gold standard, the tying of paper money to a fixed amount of gold. Harrison steadfastly refused any attempts to draw him back into running for public office, preferring to serve as an elder statesman for his party. "I do not see anything but labor and worry and distress in another campaign or in another term in the White House," he

said. With his beloved wife dead and his children living their own lives, Harrison often found himself personally adrift. "It is fearfully lonesome in this empty house," he wrote to Mary Dimmick, with whom he had maintained his close friendship. "I have not gotten into visiting habits & it is very rare that any one comes in, so my evenings are spent alone—with a book or in none too cheerful reverie."

Harrison shocked many, especially his children, by announcing over the Christmas season in 1895 his engagement to

Mary Dimmick shortly before her marriage to Harrison.

The Harrisons pose in the upstairs sitting room at their home on North Delaware Street in Indianapolis, 1896.

Dimmick, twenty-five years his junior. The couple married at Saint Thomas Episcopal Church in New York City on April 6, 1896, with Harrison's former secretary of the navy, Benjamin F. Tracy, serving as best man. Upon their return to Indianapolis after the wedding, Harrison became, due to his wife's interests, more engaged in the city's social life, attending parties and concerts. "I am not devoted to music," he said, "but Mrs. Harrison is, and I am devoted to her."

Both Russell and Mary were upset by their father's decision to remarry, and they did not attend the wedding, disapproving of the match. Writing Russell after his engagement to Dimmick had been announced in late 1895, Harrison explained his decision:

It is natural that a man's former children should not be pleased ordinarily, with a second marriage. It would not have been possible for me to marry one I did not very highly respect and very warmly love. But my life now, and much more as I grow older, is and will be a very lonely one and I cannot go on as now. A home is life's essential to me and it must be the old home. Neither of my children live here—nor are they likely to do so, and I am sure they will not wish me to live the years that remain to me in solitude.

Unfortunately, neither Russell nor his sister ever reconciled themselves to their father's marriage to Dimmick, and they remained estranged from the couple until Harrison's death. "We have done all we could, save to give each other up to please them and that no one had a right to ask," Harrison wrote Dimmick. On February 21, 1897, Dimmick gave birth to a daughter, Elizabeth, named after both their mothers.

Although Harrison campaigned on behalf of successful Republican presidential nominee William McKinley in the 1896 election, making forty speeches in Indiana, he did not always see eye to eye with the expansionist policy pursued by the administration, particularly the acquisition of Puerto Rico, the Philippines, and Guam. Harrison supported the country's involvement in the Spanish-American War, because the people of Cuba were being subjugated by Spain, calling it a "war for humanity . . . for the oppressed of another race. We could not escape this conflict." He warned, however, that the United States should "dare not say that we have God's commission to deliver the oppressed the world around." Later, Harrison refused to rejoice "in the acquisition of lands and forests and mines and commerce, at the cost of the abandonment of the old American idea that a government of absolute powers is an intolerable thing, and, under the Constitution of the United States, an impossible thing."

When McKinley stood for re-election in 1900, Harrison bowed out of doing any campaigning. "I began to make Republican speeches the year I began to vote," he told a reporter, "and have had a laborious, if

unimportant, part in every campaign, State and national, until 1898."
Although few men had made more speeches for his party than he had, and
no ex-president had made more, he had made up his mind following the
1896 election, in which he had submitted himself to "very hard usage," to
refrain from entering any more political frays. "In a word," said Harrison,
"I have vacated the choir loft and take a seat in the pews—with a deep
sense of gratitude to my forbearing fellow citizens." Still, he remained a
Republican to the end, praising the economic prosperity the country had
experienced under McKinley and denouncing the Democratic candidate,
Bryan, whose election, Harrison warned, would "throw governmental and
business affairs into confusion."

Although some in politics were surprised that a Republican of
Harrison's stature would offer such lukewarm support to a president of his
own party, his principled stand impressed some, including noted Kansas
newspaper editor William Allen White, who believed Harrison did not
seem to be "bound up in the gratification of his own ambition." White
admired Harrison's straightforwardness, noting he always spoke his mind
before becoming president, and did not change that habit after leaving
office. "He realized that the people and the wind are fickle and that election
results have little to do with the justice of any cause," wrote White, "nor
with its ultimate success or failure. He used the best means at hand in a
civilized world to find out what was right, and if he happened to believe the
politicians and people wrong, that was their affair."

Harrison always kept in his mind the belief that a president should not
carry his title with him when he retired from office. "There may be many
judges and Majors," Harrison said, "but there cannot be two Presidents."
In his book *This Country of Ours*, he recalled an anecdote involving an
unnamed president (probably himself) returning home after a hunting
trip and dressed "in a costume embodying no hint of the dignified position

BENJAMIN HARRISON PRESIDENTIAL SITE

Harrison, seen here in a circa 1900 photograph, refused to seek political office after his presidency ended. "The repugnance to further public service," he told a friend, "deepens with me every day."

he had held." A fellow traveler approached the man and asked if, "Is this President——?" The former president balked at responding, noting he was merely a fellow citizen. "The countenance of the questioner fell as she begged pardon and returned to her seat," Harrison wrote. "But the rather boisterous laughter of some young folks, who had taken in the situation, slowly revealed it to her, and she came forward to say: 'Well, I want to shake hands with you even if you ain't President now.'"

Near the end of 1897 and the beginning of 1898 Harrison had agreed to take on a case that pressed his legal talent to the fullest—representing the country of Venezuela in a border dispute with Great Britain involving its colony in Guiana. "I have given myself so absolutely and so constantly to the case of Venezuela since my appointment that I have felt recently as if I was on the verge of a breakdown," Harrison wrote a Venezuelan diplomat in Washington, D.C., in 1899. "For one year now I have taken no rest and have not even had the diversion that would have come from other professional engagements."

Over the course of five days Harrison presented his case to a five-man International Arbitration Tribunal convened in Paris, France. Writing his old attorney general and friend William H. H. Miller, Harrison said he had made a valiant effort to "put the hearing purely upon an impartial, judicial basis, but there are two Britons in the panel—men who sitting as judges in an ordinary case would be absolutely impartial and just. But the idea of representation has prevailed in these tribunals and I fear will do so in this." His fears were justified; the tribunal gave nearly all of the contested territory to Great Britain. "Law is nothing to a British judge it seems when it is a matter of extending British domination," Harrison complained to Miller.

The illness that took Harrison's life came as a surprise to him and his family. It happened in early March 1901. On the morning of March 7, Harrison, who had recently recovered from a cold, took his usual walk and prepared to visit the law library for help with a case he was working on and expected to argue before the Supreme Court in a few weeks. He and his wife had breakfast together and Harrison had retired to his library to read the newspaper. Frank Tibbott, his personal secretary, came down from his room at about 9:00 a.m. and met Harrison in the hallway. "He bade me good morning and said 'We will go down to the law library presently,'" Tibbott recalled. About a half hour later, Mary heard her husband call to her in a startled voice, and when she went to him she saw him sitting before the fire. "I am having a dreadful chill," he said. A doctor was called to the scene and Harrison went to bed at about 11:00 a.m. "He [Harrison] said to me then 'this could not have been more sudden if someone had hit me on the head with a hammer,'" said Tibbott.

Various doctors and nurses attended to Harrison over the next few days and administered oxygen as his grippe (influenza) developed into pneumonia. Visited by his daughter, Elizabeth, Harrison rallied for a time, telling her, "I would give $100 if I could take a walk with you today!" Mary, who remained constantly by her husband's side during his illness, remembered that her husband's mind began to wander. "He seemed troubled over some public affairs, and I said to him—'dear, don't worry over these things, they will come out all right.' He would rouse himself and say 'I cannot get these things out of my mind, you do not know how many things are passing through my mind,'" she recalled. The sixty-seven-year-old Harrison died at 4:45 p.m. on March 13.

On March 16 pallbearers took Harrison's body from his home to lay in state in the rotunda at the Indiana Statehouse, where thousands of his fellow citizens, including surviving members of his old Civil War regiment, the Seventieth Indiana, paid their respects. "There were not many of these veterans—less than a hundred—but each one stood for a little group lying

INDIANA HISTORICAL SOCIETY

A carriage waits to take Harrison's body from his home to lie in state in the rotunda of the Indiana Statehouse.

somewhere beneath the friendly sod," reported the *Indianapolis Journal*. "Doubtless memories of other fallen comrades than the one upon whose face they looked mingled with those evoked by the sight of their leader lying pale and cold and majestic in death, for there was not a dry eye in the group and many a bent form shook with the depth of emotion only age can feel."

With President McKinley in attendance, funeral services were held the following day at First Presbyterian Church, with burial following at Crown Hill Cemetery alongside the grave of his first wife, Caroline. Also gathered for the services were former members of Harrison's cabinet, the ex-president's

Harrison's funeral procession arrives at the Indiana Statehouse.

INDIANA HISTORICAL SOCIETY

Interior of Indianapolis's First Presbyterian Church before Harrison's funeral on March 17, 1901.

family members, and numerous U.S. senators and state governors. In his proclamation announcing Harrison's death, McKinley praised his fellow Republican for his "extraordinary gifts as administrator and statesman. In public and in private life he set a shining example for his countrymen."

Hoosiers everywhere mourned the loss of a man Indiana governor Winfield T. Durbin called the state's "most distinguished citizen." Public businesses were closed for the day of Harrison's funeral and all flags were placed at half-staff. Among the many tributes published about the former president, one that stood out was offered by his biographer and best-selling author Lew Wallace. "He had every quality of greatness—a courage that was dauntless, foresight almost to prophecy, a mind clear, strong, and of breadth by nature, strengthened by exercise and constant dealing with subjects of National import, subjects of world-wide interest," Wallace said of his longtime friend. "And of these qualities the people knew, and they

LIBRARY OF CONGRESS

Harrison monument at Crown Hill Cemetery, with smaller markers at its base for the ex-president and his first wife, Caroline Scott Harrison.

drew them to him as listeners and believers, and in the faith they brought him there was no mixture of doubt or fear."

Harrison had always done well for Indianapolis, and the city stood by its favorite son in the years following his death with monuments to his memory. In 1906 construction began on a new U.S. Army fort located in the small town of Lawrence, Indiana, located a few miles northeast of Indianapolis, which was named in honor of the twenty-third president. On October 27, 1908, a statue of him sculpted by Charles Henry Niehaus was unveiled to the public at University Park, the location where Harrison had given so many impromptu speeches during his 1888 presidential campaign. Harrison's eleven-year-old daughter, Elizabeth, pulled the chord that revealed the bronze statue to the waiting crowd. Etched on the south front of the statue's limestone base after Harrison's name are the words: "A Citizen Faithful to Every Obligation / A Lawyer of Distinction / A Volunteer Soldier in the War for the Union / A Senator in Congress / The Twenty-Third President of the United States."

The location that has drawn the most attention to Harrison's legacy is his home at 1230 North Delaware Street, today operated as the nonprofit Benjamin Harrison Presidential Site. When he returned after his service in the White House, Harrison had made some renovations to his house, including adding a front porch, wiring the home for electricity, and updating the plumbing. After Harrison's death, his wife and daughter continued to live at the residence until 1913, when they moved to New York City (Mary Dimmick Harrison died on January 5, 1948, and was buried at Crown Hill next to her husband). For a number of years the house was rented out to families and also served as a rooming house. In March 1937 the Arthur Jordan Foundation bought the house, plus its furniture, and used the structure as a dormitory for female students in the Jordan Conservatory of Music. As part of its purchase agreement with Mary, the

Elizabeth Harrison checks out a piece of art during a visit to the studio of sculptor Charles Henry Niehaus, who in the background works on a model of his sculpture of her father.

foundation agreed that the home would be considered a memorial to her late husband.

With the music school's move to Butler University in 1951, the Harrison home was finally opened to the public. Thirteen years later, the U.S. Department of the Interior declared the house a National Historic Landmark. Accredited by the American Association of Museums, the site today strives to "share the life stories, arts and culture of an American President to increase public participation in the American system of self-government." The home offers guided tours to the public and school groups and hosts exhibitions and programs on different aspects of Harrison's career and the presidency.

Elizabeth Harrison walks away after unveiling the statue honoring her father at Indianapolis's University Park.

Contemporary view of the Benjamin Harrison Presidential Site in Indianapolis, including a state
historical marker in his honor.

Unfortunately, on a national level, Harrison's presidential legacy received
scant attention following his death through a strange twist of events.
Although fellow Hoosier Republican Charles W. Fairbanks, who served as vice
president under Theodore Roosevelt, had confidently stated that Harrison
would stand as one of the country's great presidents when his life had been
"impartially written," such a task proved difficult to accomplish. Harrison's
first would-be biographer, Tibbott, started his work in 1901, but gave up the
job three years later. Tibbott turned over material on Harrison to John L.
Griffiths, an Indiana lawyer who expected to finish his work in less than two
years. Griffiths, however, often had his work interrupted by a distinguished
diplomatic career, and died in 1914 with the biography still unwritten.

As Harrison's widow searched for someone to take over the project, she deposited the ex-president's papers with the Library of Congress, granting no access to them by researchers without her permission. A number of potential writers were considered, including James A. Woodburn, a distinguished professor of history at Indiana University, but it took until late 1926 before an official biographer was announced—A. T. Volwiler, a Wittenberg College professor, who worked on the project for the next nineteen years without producing a biography. A year after Mary Dimmick Harrison's death in 1948, Harry J. Sievers, head of the history department at Bellarmine College in Plattsburgh, New York, accepted a commission from the Arthur Jordan Foundation finally to write a definitive biography of Harrison—a task he accomplished in three volumes published in 1952, 1959, and 1968.

Not surprisingly, with no champion singing his praises, Harrison has suffered when it came to the ranking of his presidency by historians, falling in the middle of the pack and even lower. In recent years, however, his time in the White House has received greater respect from historians as being a forerunner of the modern presidency—a position often credited to McKinley. "In his own right," noted historian Charles Calhoun, who produced the best modern book on the Harrison administration, "Harrison made important contributions to the evolution of the office. He entered the presidency strongly committed to a sense of principles and policies. In defense of those ideas and in pursuit of what he thought to be his duty, he expanded the boundaries of presidential activism."

Most one-term presidents are judged to be political failures, because their administrations have been rejected by voters at the polls. Harrison, however, left behind a solid record of which any statesman would be proud. During four years in the White House, he preserved millions of acres of national forests, fought on behalf of African American voting

In 1933 a presidential historian predicted that when Harrison was viewed "in true historical perspective he will appear larger and more important than he now does."

rights, modernized the U.S. Navy, began the push to restrain large business trusts, and strengthened American trade with other countries in the Western Hemisphere. For Harrison, what might have mattered most was the dedication and respect he held for the office of president. "Those who would associate their names with events that shall outlive a century can only do so by high consecration to duty," he said. "Self-seeking has no public observance or anniversary."

Benjamin Harrison's Inaugural Address

Fellow-Citizens:

There is no constitutional or legal requirement that the President shall take the oath of office in the presence of the people, but there is so manifest an appropriateness in the public induction to office of the chief executive officer of the nation that from the beginning of the Government the people, to whose service the official oath consecrates the officer, have been called to witness the solemn ceremonial. The oath taken in the presence of the people becomes a mutual covenant. The officer covenants to serve the whole body of the people by a faithful execution of the laws, so that they may be the unfailing defense and security of those who respect and observe them, and that neither wealth, station, nor the power of combinations shall be able to evade their just penalties or to wrest them from a beneficent public purpose to serve the ends of cruelty or selfishness.

My promise is spoken; yours unspoken, but not the less real and solemn. The people of every State have here their representatives. Surely I do not misinterpret the spirit of the occasion when I assume that the whole body of the people covenant with me and with each other to-day to support and defend the Constitution and the Union of the States, to yield willing obedience to all the laws and each to every other citizen his equal civil and political rights. Entering thus solemnly into covenant with each other, we may reverently invoke and confidently expect the favor and help of Almighty God—that He will give to me wisdom, strength, and fidelity, and to our people a spirit of fraternity and a love of righteousness and peace.

This occasion derives peculiar interest from the fact that the Presidential term which begins this day is the twenty-sixth under our

Constitution. The first inauguration of President Washington took place in New York, where Congress was then sitting, on the 30th day of April, 1789, having been deferred by reason of delays attending the organization of the Congress and the canvass of the electoral vote. Our people have already worthily observed the centennials of the Declaration of Independence, of the battle of Yorktown, and of the adoption of the Constitution, and will shortly celebrate in New York the institution of the second great department of our constitutional scheme of government. When the centennial of the institution of the judicial department, by the organization of the Supreme Court, shall have been suitably observed, as I trust it will be, our nation will have fully entered its second century.

I will not attempt to note the marvelous and in great part happy contrasts between our country as it steps over the threshold into its second century of organized existence under the Constitution and that weak but wisely ordered young nation that looked undauntedly down the first century, when all its years stretched out before it.

Our people will not fail at this time to recall the incidents which accompanied the institution of government under the Constitution, or to find inspiration and guidance in the teachings and example of Washington and his great associates, and hope and courage in the contrast which thirty-eight populous and prosperous States offer to the thirteen States, weak in everything except courage and the love of liberty, that then fringed our Atlantic seaboard.

The Territory of Dakota has now a population greater than any of the original States (except Virginia) and greater than the aggregate of five of the smaller States in 1790. The center of population when our national capital was located was east of Baltimore, and it was argued by many well-informed persons that it would move eastward rather than westward; yet in 1880 it was found to be near Cincinnati, and the new census about to be taken will show another stride to the westward. That which was the body has come to be only the rich fringe of the nation's robe. But our growth has not been limited to territory, population and aggregate wealth, marvelous as it has been in each of those directions. The masses of our people are better fed, clothed, and housed than their fathers were. The facilities for popular education have been vastly enlarged and more generally diffused.

The virtues of courage and patriotism have given recent proof of their continued presence and increasing power in the hearts and over the lives of our people. The influences of religion have been multiplied and strengthened. The sweet offices of charity have greatly increased. The virtue of temperance is held in higher estimation. We have not attained an ideal condition. Not all of our people are happy and prosperous; not all of them are virtuous and law-abiding. But on the whole the opportunities offered to the individual to secure the comforts of life are better than are found elsewhere and largely better than they were here one hundred years ago.

The surrender of a large measure of sovereignty to the General Government, effected by the adoption of the Constitution, was not accomplished until the suggestions of reason were strongly reenforced by the more imperative voice of experience. The divergent interests of peace speedily demanded a "more perfect union." The merchant, the shipmaster, and the manufacturer discovered and disclosed to our statesmen and to the people that commercial emancipation must be added to the political freedom which had been so bravely won. The commercial policy of the mother country had not relaxed any of its hard and oppressive features. To hold in check the development of our commercial marine, to prevent or retard the establishment and growth of manufactures in the States, and so to secure the American market for their shops and the carrying trade for their ships, was the policy of European statesmen, and was pursued with the most selfish vigor.

Petitions poured in upon Congress urging the imposition of
discriminating duties that should encourage the production of needed
things at home. The patriotism of the people, which no longer found afield
of exercise in war, was energetically directed to the duty of equipping the
young Republic for the defense of its independence by making its people
self-dependent. Societies for the promotion of home manufactures and
for encouraging the use of domestics in the dress of the people were
organized in many of the States. The revival at the end of the century of the
same patriotic interest in the preservation and development of domestic
industries and the defense of our working people against injurious foreign
competition is an incident worthy of attention. It is not a departure
but a return that we have witnessed. The protective policy had then its
opponents. The argument was made, as now, that its benefits inured to
particular classes or sections.

If the question became in any sense or at any time sectional, it was
only because slavery existed in some of the States. But for this there was
no reason why the cotton-producing States should not have led or walked
abreast with the New England States in the production of cotton fabrics.
There was this reason only why the States that divide with Pennsylvania
the mineral treasures of the great southeastern and central mountain
ranges should have been so tardy in bringing to the smelting furnace and to
the mill the coal and iron from their near opposing hillsides. Mill fires were
lighted at the funeral pile of slavery. The emancipation proclamation was
heard in the depths of the earth as well as in the sky; men were made free,
and material things became our better servants.

The sectional element has happily been eliminated from the tariff
discussion. We have no longer States that are necessarily only planting
States. None are excluded from achieving that diversification of pursuits
among the people which brings wealth and contentment. The cotton

plantation will not be less valuable when the product is spun in the country town by operatives whose necessities call for diversified crops and create a home demand for garden and agricultural products. Every new mine, furnace, and factory is an extension of the productive capacity of the State more real and valuable than added territory.

Shall the prejudices and paralysis of slavery continue to hang upon the skirts of progress? How long will those who rejoice that slavery no longer exists cherish or tolerate the incapacities it put upon their communities? I look hopefully to the continuance of our protective system and to the consequent development of manufacturing and mining enterprises in the States hitherto wholly given to agriculture as a potent influence in the perfect unification of our people. The men who have invested their capital in these enterprises, the farmers who have felt the benefit of their neighborhood, and the men who work in shop or field will not fail to find and to defend a community of interest.

Is it not quite possible that the farmers and the promoters of the great mining and manufacturing enterprises which have recently been established in the South may yet find that the free ballot of the workingman, without distinction of race, is needed for their defense as well as for his own? I do not doubt that if those men in the South who now accept the tariff views of Clay and the constitutional expositions of Webster would courageously avow and defend their real convictions they would not find it difficult, by friendly instruction and cooperation, to make the black man their efficient and safe ally, not only in establishing correct principles in our national administration, but in preserving for their local communities the benefits of social order and economical and honest government. At least until the good offices of kindness and education have been fairly tried the contrary conclusion can not be plausibly urged.

THE NEW ADMINISTRATION.—VISITORS PAYING THEIR RESPECTS TO PRESIDENT HARRISON
AT THE WHITE HOUSE.
SEE PAGE 90.

*Drawing showing visitors paying their respects to President Benjamin Harrison at the White House
following his inauguration in 1889.*

I have altogether rejected the suggestion of a special Executive policy for any section of our country. It is the duty of the Executive to administer and enforce in the methods and by the instrumentalities pointed out and provided by the Constitution all the laws enacted by Congress. These laws are general and their administration should be uniform and equal. As a citizen may not elect what laws he will obey, neither may the Executive eject which he will enforce. The duty to obey and to execute embraces the Constitution in its entirety and the whole code of laws enacted under it. The evil example of permitting individuals, corporations, or communities to nullify the laws because they cross some selfish or local interest or prejudices is full of danger, not only to the nation at large, but much more to those who use this pernicious expedient to escape their just obligations or to obtain an unjust advantage over others. They will presently themselves be compelled to appeal to the law for protection, and those who would use the law as a defense must not deny that use of it to others.

If our great corporations would more scrupulously observe their legal limitations and duties, they would have less cause to complain of the unlawful limitations of their rights or of violent interference with their operations. The community that by concert, open or secret, among its citizens denies to a portion of its members their plain rights under the law has severed the only safe bond of social order and prosperity. The evil works from a bad center both ways. It demoralizes those who practice it and destroys the faith of those who suffer by it in the efficiency of the law as a safe protector. The man in whose breast that faith has been darkened is naturally the subject of dangerous and uncanny suggestions. Those who use unlawful methods, if moved by no higher motive than the selfishness that prompted them, may well stop and inquire what is to be the end of this.

An unlawful expedient can not become a permanent condition of government. If the educated and influential classes in a community either practice or connive at the systematic violation of laws that seem to them to cross their convenience, what can they expect when the lesson that convenience or a supposed class interest is a sufficient cause for lawlessness has been well learned by the ignorant classes? A community where law is the rule of conduct and where courts, not mobs, execute its penalties is the only attractive field for business investments and honest labor.

Our naturalization laws should be so amended as to make the inquiry into the character and good disposition of persons applying for citizenship more careful and searching. Our existing laws have been in their administration an unimpressive and often an unintelligible form. We accept the man as a citizen without any knowledge of his fitness, and he assumes the duties of citizenship without any knowledge as to what they are. The privileges of American citizenship are so great and its duties so grave that we may well insist upon a good knowledge of every person applying for citizenship and a good knowledge by him of our institutions. We should not cease to be hospitable to immigration, but we should cease to be careless as to the character of it. There are men of all races, even the best, whose coming is necessarily a burden upon our public revenues or a threat to social order. These should be identified and excluded.

We have happily maintained a policy of avoiding all interference with European affairs. We have been only interested spectators of their contentions in diplomacy and in war, ready to use our friendly offices to promote peace, but never obtruding our advice and never attempting unfairly to coin the distresses of other powers into commercial advantage to ourselves. We have a just right to expect that our European policy will be the American policy of European courts.

It is so manifestly incompatible with those precautions for our peace and safety which all the great powers habitually observe and enforce in matters affecting them that a shorter waterway between our eastern and western seaboards should be dominated by any European Government that we may confidently expect that such a purpose will not be entertained by any friendly power.

We shall in the future, as in the past, use every endeavor to maintain and enlarge our friendly relations with all the great powers, but they will not expect us to look kindly upon any project that would leave us subject to the dangers of a hostile observation or environment. We have not sought to dominate or to absorb any of our weaker neighbors, but rather to aid and encourage them to establish free and stable governments resting upon the consent of their own people. We have a clear right to expect, therefore, that no European Government will seek to establish colonial dependencies upon the territory of these independent American States. That which a sense of justice restrains us from seeking they may be reasonably expected willingly to forego.

It must not be assumed, however, that our interests are so exclusively American that our entire inattention to any events that may transpire elsewhere can be taken for granted. Our citizens domiciled for purposes of trade in all countries and in many of the islands of the sea demand and will have our adequate care in their personal and commercial rights. The necessities of our Navy require convenient coaling stations and dock and harbor privileges. These and other trading privileges we will feel free to obtain only by means that do not in any degree partake of coercion, however feeble the government from which we ask such concessions. But having fairly obtained them by methods and for purposes entirely consistent with the most friendly disposition toward all other powers, our consent will be necessary to any modification or impairment of the concession.

We shall neither fail to respect the flag of any friendly nation or the just rights of its citizens, nor to exact the like treatment for our own. Calmness, justice, and consideration should characterize our diplomacy. The offices of an intelligent diplomacy or of friendly arbitration in proper cases should be adequate to the peaceful adjustment of all international difficulties. By such methods we will make our contribution to the world's peace, which no nation values more highly, and avoid the opprobrium which must fall upon the nation that ruthlessly breaks it.

The duty devolved by law upon the President to nominate and, by and with the advice and consent of the Senate, to appoint all public officers whose appointment is not otherwise provided for in the Constitution or by act of Congress has become very burdensome and its wise and efficient discharge full of difficulty. The civil list is so large that a personal knowledge of any large number of the applicants is impossible. The President must rely upon the representations of others, and these are often made inconsiderately and without any just sense of responsibility. I have a right, I think, to insist that those who volunteer or are invited to give advice as to appointments shall exercise consideration and fidelity. A high sense of duty and an ambition to improve the service should characterize all public officers.

There are many ways in which the convenience and comfort of those who have business with our public offices may be promoted by a thoughtful and obliging officer, and I shall expect those whom I may appoint to justify their selection by a conspicuous efficiency in the discharge of their duties. Honorable party service will certainly not be esteemed by me a disqualification for public office, but it will in no case be allowed to serve as a shield of official negligence, incompetency, or delinquency. It is entirely creditable to seek public office by proper methods and with proper motives, and all applicants will be treated with consideration; but I shall need, and

Couples dance at Harrison's inaugural ball, held at the Pension Building.

the heads of Departments will need, time for inquiry and deliberation. Persistent importunity will not, therefore, be the best support of an application for office. Heads of Departments, bureaus, and all other public officers having any duty connected therewith will be expected to enforce the civil-service law fully and without evasion. Beyond this obvious duty I hope to do something more to advance the reform of the civil service. The ideal, or even my own ideal, I shall probably not attain. Retrospect will be a safer basis of judgment than promises. We shall not, however, I am sure, be able to put our civil service upon a nonpartisan basis until we have secured an incumbency that fair-minded men of the opposition will approve for impartiality and integrity. As the number of such in the civil list is increased removals from office will diminish.

While a Treasury surplus is not the greatest evil, it is a serious evil. Our revenue should be ample to meet the ordinary annual demands upon our Treasury, with a sufficient margin for those extraordinary but scarcely less imperative demands which arise now and then. Expenditure should always be made with economy and only upon public necessity. Wastefulness, profligacy, or favoritism in public expenditures is criminal. But there is nothing in the condition of our country or of our people to suggest that anything presently necessary to the public prosperity, security, or honor should be unduly postponed.

It will be the duty of Congress wisely to forecast and estimate these extraordinary demands, and, having added them to our ordinary expenditures, to so adjust our revenue laws that no considerable annual surplus will remain. We will fortunately be able to apply to the redemption of the public debt any small and unforeseen excess of revenue. This is better than to reduce our income below our necessary expenditures, with the resulting choice between another change of our revenue laws and an increase of the public debt. It is quite possible, I am sure, to effect the necessary reduction in our revenues without breaking down our protective tariff or seriously injuring any domestic industry.

The construction of a sufficient number of modern war ships and of their necessary armament should progress as rapidly as is consistent with care and perfection in plans and workmanship. The spirit, courage, and skill of our naval officers and seamen have many times in our history given to weak ships and inefficient guns a rating greatly beyond that of the naval list. That they will again do so upon occasion I do not doubt; but they ought not, by premeditation or neglect, to be left to the risks and exigencies of an unequal combat. We should encourage the establishment of American steamship lines. The exchanges of commerce demand stated, reliable, and rapid means of communication, and until these are provided the development of our trade with the States lying south of us is impossible.

Our pension laws should give more adequate and discriminating relief to the Union soldiers and sailors and to their widows and orphans. Such occasions as this should remind us that we owe everything to their valor and sacrifice.

It is a subject of congratulation that there is a near prospect of the admission into the Union of the Dakotas and Montana and Washington Territories. This act of justice has been unreasonably delayed in the case of some of them. The people who have settled these Territories are intelligent, enterprising, and patriotic, and the accession these new States will add strength to the nation. It is due to the settlers in the Territories who have availed themselves of the invitations of our land laws to make homes upon the public domain that their titles should be speedily adjusted and their honest entries confirmed by patent.

It is very gratifying to observe the general interest now being manifested in the reform of our election laws. Those who have been for years calling attention to the pressing necessity of throwing about the ballot box and about the elector further safeguards, in order that our elections might not only be free and pure, but might clearly appear to be so, will welcome the accession of any who did not so soon discover the need of reform. The National Congress has not as yet taken control of elections in that case over which the Constitution gives it jurisdiction, but has accepted and adopted the election laws of the several States, provided penalties for their violation and a method of supervision. Only the inefficiency of the State laws or an unfair partisan administration of them could suggest a departure from this policy.

It was clearly, however, in the contemplation of the framers of the Constitution that such an exigency might arise, and provision was wisely made for it. The freedom of the ballot is a condition of our national life, and no power vested in Congress or in the Executive to secure or perpetuate it should remain unused upon occasion. The people of all the Congressional districts have an equal interest that the election in each shall truly express the views and wishes of a majority of the qualified electors residing within it. The results of such elections are not local, and the insistence of electors residing in other districts that they shall be pure and free does not savor at all of impertinence.

If in any of the States the public security is thought to be threatened by ignorance among the electors, the obvious remedy is education. The sympathy and help of our people will not be withheld from any community struggling with special embarrassments or difficulties connected with the suffrage if the remedies proposed proceed upon lawful lines and are promoted by just and honorable methods. How shall those who practice election frauds recover that respect for the sanctity of the ballot which is the first condition and obligation of good citizenship? The man who has come to regard the ballot box as a juggler's hat has renounced his allegiance.

Let us exalt patriotism and moderate our party contentions. Let those who would die for the flag on the field of battle give a better proof of their patriotism and a higher glory to their country by promoting fraternity and justice. A party success that is achieved by unfair methods or by practices that partake of revolution is hurtful and evanescent even from a party standpoint. We should hold our differing opinions in mutual respect, and, having submitted them to the arbitrament of the ballot, should accept an adverse judgment with the same respect that we would have demanded of our opponents if the decision had been in our favor.

No other people have a government more worthy of their respect and love or a land so magnificent in extent, so pleasant to look upon, and so full of generous suggestion to enterprise and labor. God has placed upon our head a diadem and has laid at our feet power and wealth beyond definition or calculation. But we must not forget that we take these gifts upon the condition that justice and mercy shall hold the reins of power and that the upward avenues of hope shall be free to all the people.

I do not mistrust the future. Dangers have been in frequent ambush along our path, but we have uncovered and vanquished them all. Passion has swept some of our communities, but only to give us a new demonstration that the great body of our people are stable, patriotic, and law-abiding. No political party can long pursue advantage at the expense of public honor or by rude and indecent methods without protest and fatal disaffection in its own body. The peaceful agencies of commerce are more fully revealing the necessary unity of all our communities, and the increasing intercourse of our people is promoting mutual respect. We shall find unalloyed pleasure in the revelation which our next census will make of the swift development of the great resources of some of the States. Each State will bring its generous contribution to the great aggregate of the nation's increase. And when the harvests from the fields, the cattle from the hills, and the ores of the earth shall have been weighed, counted, and valued, we will turn from them all to crown with the highest honor the State that has most promoted education, virtue, justice, and patriotism among its people.

Benjamin Harrison Quotes

"Great lives never go out; they go on."

"If I were to select a watchword that I would have every young man write above his door and on his heart, it would be that good word 'Fidelity.' I know of no better. The man who meets every obligation to the family, to society, to the State, to his country, and his God, to the very best measure of his strength and ability, cannot fail of that assurance and quietness that comes of a good conscience, and will seldom fail of the approval of his fellow-men, and will never fail of the reward which is promised to his faithfulness."

"An American citizen could not be a good citizen who did not have hope in his heart."

"How shall one be a safe citizen when citizens are rulers who are not intelligent? How shall he understand these great questions which his suffrage must adjudge without thorough intellectual culture in his youth?"

"Equality is the golden thread that runs through all the fabric of our civil institutions—the dominating note in the swelling symphony of liberty."

"I cannot always sympathize with that demand which we hear so frequently for cheap things. Things may be too cheap. They are too cheap when the man or woman who produces them upon the farm or the man or woman who produces them in the factory does not get out of them living wages with a margin for old age and for a dowry for the incidents that are to follow. I pity the man who wants a coat so cheap that the man or woman who produces the cloth or shapes it into a garment will starve in the process."

"We cannot afford in America to have any discontented classes, and if fair wages are paid for fair work we will have none."

"We Americans have no commission from God to police the world."

"The bud of victory is always in the truth."

President Benjamin Harrison (center, sitting in chair) with group at Roseland Cottage, Woodstock, Connecticut, July 4, 1889. Other presidents who visited Roseland for large Fourth of July celebrations included Ulysses S. Grant, Rutherford B. Hayes, and William McKinley.

BENJAMIN HARRISON PRESIDENTIAL SITE

"I have a great risk of meeting a fool at home, but the candidate who travels cannot escape him."

"I have often thought the life of the President is like that of the policeman in the opera, not a happy one."

"I would a thousand times rather march under the bloody shirt, stained with the lifeblood of a Union soldier, than to march under the black flag of treason or the white flag of compromise."

"The prejudices of generations are not like marks upon the blackboard that can be rubbed out with a sponge. These are more like the deep glacial lines that the years have left in the rock, but the water, when the surface is exposed to its quiet, gentle, and perpetual influence, wears even these out, until the surface is smooth and uniform."

"The disfranchisement of a single legal elector by fraud or intimidation is a crime too grave to be regarded lightly."

"The manner by which women are treated is a good criterion to judge the true state of society. If we know but this one feature in a character of a nation, we may easily judge the rest, for as society advances, the true character of women is discovered."

"The flag can not stand for the benevolent policies of an administration. It stands for more permanent things—for things that changing administrations have no power to change."

"Perhaps no emotion cools sooner than gratitude."

"I do not know whether it is prejudice or not, but anyway I always have a very high opinion of a state whose chief production is corn."

"And we must not forget that it is often easier to assemble armies than it is to assemble army revenues."

"Unlike many other people less happy, we give our devotion to a government, to its Constitution, to its flag, and not to men."

"I believe also in the American opportunity that puts the starry sky above every boy's head, and sets his foot upon a ladder that he may climb until his strength gives out."

"Let those who would die for the flag on the field of battle give a better proof of their patriotism and a higher glory to the country by promoting fraternity and justice."

"Our mission is not to impose our peculiar institutions upon other nations by physical force or diplomatic treachery but rather by internal peace and prosperity to solve the problem of self-government and reconcile democratic freedom with national stability."

"We have not attained an ideal condition. Not all of our people are happy and prosperous; not all of them are virtuous and law-abiding. But on the whole the opportunities offered to the individual to secure the comforts of life are better than are found elsewhere and largely better than they were here one hundred years ago."

Learn More About Benjamin Harrison

Manuscript Collections

Benjamin Harrison Collection. Benjamin Harrison Presidential Site, Indianapolis, IN.

Benjamin Harrison Collection, 1853–1943, M 132. Indiana Historical Society William Henry Smith Memorial Library, Indianapolis, IN.

Benjamin Harrison Papers. Library of Congress, Washington, D.C.

Audiovisual Materials

Jim Simons, Produce/Writer. *A President at the Crossroads*. WFYI Productions and the Benjamin Harrison Presidential site. DVD. 2017.

Websites

Benjamin Harrison Presidential Site. http://www.presidentbenjaminharrison.org/.

Benjamin Harrison, U.S. Presidents. Miller Center, University of Virginia, https://millercenter .org/president/bharrison.

Benjamin Harrison, The White House. https://www.whitehouse.gov/about-the-white-house/ presidents/benjamin-harrison/.

Benjamin Harrison, HISTORY.com. http://www.history.com/topics/us-presidents/benjamin -harrison.

Articles

Abbott, Carl. "Indianapolis in the 1850s: Popular Economic Thought and Urban Growth." *Indiana Magazine of History* 74 (December 1978): 293–315.

Barry, Peter J. "*Ex parte Milligan*: History and Historians." *Indiana Magazine of History* 109 (December 2013): 355–79.

Boomhower, Ray E. "'To Secure Honest Elections': Jacob Piatt Dunn, Jr. and the Reform of Indiana's Ballot." *Indiana Magazine of History* 90 (December 1994): 311–45.

Bourdon, Jeffrey Normand. "Trains, Canes, and Replica Log Cabins: Benjamin Harrison's 1888 Front-Porch Campaign for the Presidency." *Indiana Magazine of History* 110 (September 2014): 246–69.

Buley, R. C. "The Campaign of 1888 in Indiana." *Indiana Magazine of History* 10 (June 1914): 30–53.

Dozer, Donald Marquand. "Benjamin Harrison and the Presidential Campaign of 1892." *American Historical Review* 54 (October 1948): 49–77.

Frantz, Edward. "A March of Triumph? Benjamin Harrison's Southern Tour and the Limits of Racial and Regional Reconciliation." *Indiana Magazine of History* 100 (December 2004): 293–320.

Fischer, Roger A. "'Blocks of Five' Dudley, Cartoon Celebrity." *Indiana Magazine of History* 87 (December 1991): 334–47.

Halford, E. W. "General Harrison's Attitude Toward the Presidency." *Century Magazine* 85 (June 1912): 305–10.

Hoover, Irwin H. (Ike). "Presidents Are People." *Saturday Evening Post*, March 3, 1934.

Kinzer, Donald L. "Benjamin Harrison and the Politics of Availability." In Ralph D. Gray, ed. *Gentlemen from Indiana: National Party Candidates, 1836–1940.* Indianapolis: Indiana Historical Bureau, 1977.

Lindgren, Jim. "Public Interest and Public Order: Indianapolis and the Great Strike of 1877." *Traces of Indiana and Midwestern History* 21 (Fall 2009): 42–51.

"Mr. Vice President's Brush with the Law." *Wabash Magazine* (Winter 1999), https://www.wabash.edu/magazine/1999/winter/features/vicepresident.htm/.

Sinkler, George. "Benjamin Harrison and the Matter of Race." *Indiana Magazine of History* 65 (September 1969): 197–214.

Spetter, Allan Burton. "Benjamin Harrison." In John A. Garraty and Mark C. Carnes, eds. *American National Biography*, vol. 10. New York: Oxford University Press, 1999.

———. "Harrison and Blaine: Foreign Policy, 1889–1893." *Indiana Magazine of History* 65 (September 1969): 215–27.

Towne, Stephen E. "The Persistent Nullifier: The Life of Civil War Conspirator Lambdin P. Milligan." *Indiana Magazine of History* 109 (December 2013): 303–54.

Williams, John Alexander. "Stephen B. Elkins and the Benjamin Harrison Campaign and Cabinet, 1887–1891." *Indiana Magazine of History* 68 (March 1972): 1–23.

Books

Boller, Paul F., Jr. *Presidential Campaigns.* New York: Oxford University Press, 1984.

———. *Presidential Wives: An Anecdotal History.* New York: Oxford University Press, 1988.

Boomhower, Ray E. *Jacob Piatt Dunn, Jr.: A Life in History and Politics, 1855–1924*. Indianapolis: Indiana Historical Society, 1997.

Bower, Stephen E. *The American Army in the Heartland: A History of Fort Benjamin Harrison, 1903–1995*. Fort Benjamin Harrison, IN: Command History Office, U.S. Army Soldier Support Center, 1995.

Brown, Dee. *Bury My Heart at Wounded Knee: An Indian History of the American West*. New York: Henry Holt and Company, 1970.

Calhoun, Charles W. *Benjamin Harrison*. New York: Times, 2005.

———. *From Bloody Shirt to Full Dinner Pail: The Transformation of Politics and Governance in the Gilded Age*. New York: Hill and Wang, 2010.

———. *Minority Victory: Gilded Age Politics and the Front Porch Campaign of 1888*. Lawrence: University Press of Kansas, 2008.

Cavinder, Fred D. *The Indiana Book of Quotes*. Indianapolis: Indiana Historical Society Press, 2005.

Cherny, Robert W. *American Politics in the Gilded Age, 1868–1900*. Wheeling, IL: Harlan Davidson, 1997.

Graff, Henry F. *Grover Cleveland*. New York: Times Books, 2002.

Gray, Ralph D. *Indiana's Favorite Sons, 1840–1940*. Indianapolis: Indiana Historical Society, 1988.

Greene, Jerome A. *American Carnage: Wounded Knee, 1890*. Norman: University of Oklahoma Press, 2014.

Gresham, Matilda. *Life of Walter Q. Gresham*. 2 vols. Chicago: Rand McNally and Company, 1919.

Harrison, Benjamin. *This Country of Ours*. New York: Charles Scribner, 1897.

———. *Views of an Ex-President: Being His Addresses and Writings on Subjects of Public Interest since the Close of his Administration as President of the United States*. Compiled by Mary Lord Harrison. Indianapolis, IN: Bowen-Merrill Company, 1901.

Hays, Samuel P. *The Response to Industrialism, 1885–1914*. Chicago: University of Chicago Press, 1957.

Jensen, Richard J. *The Winning of the Midwest: Social and Political Conflict, 1888–96*. Chicago: University of Chicago Press, 1971.

Josephson, Matthew. *The Politicos, 1865–1919*. New York: Harcourt, Brace, 1938.

Kehl, James A. *Boss Rule in the Gilded Age: Matt Quay of Pennsylvania*. Pittsburgh: University of Pittsburgh Press, 1981.

Knoles, George H. *The Presidential Campaign and Election of 1892*. Palo Alto, CA: Stanford University Press, 1942.

Marshall, Thomas R. *Recollections of Thomas R. Marshall, Vice-President and Hoosier Philosopher: A Hoosier Salad*. Indianapolis: Bobbs-Merrill Company, 1925.

McPherson, James M. *Battle Cry of Freedom: The Civil War Era*. New York: Oxford University Press, 1988.

Morsberger, Robert E., and Katharine M. *Lew Wallace: Militant Romantic*. New York: McGraw-Hill, 1980.

Muzzey, David Saville. *James G. Blaine: A Political Idol of Other Days*. New York: Dodd, Mead and Company, 1934.

Nevins, Allan. *Grover Cleveland: A Study in Courage*. New York: Dodd, Mead and Company, 1933.

Phillips, Clifton J. *Indiana in Transition: The Emergence of an Industrial Commonwealth, 1880–1920*. Indianapolis: Indiana Historical Bureau, 1968.

Report of Benjamin Harrison Memorial Commission (Seventy-Seventh Congress, First Session, House Document Number 154). Washington, D.C.: Government Printing Office, 1941.

Richardson, Heather Cox. *To Make Men Free: A History of the Republican Party*. New York: Basic Books, 2014.

Sievers, Harry J. *Benjamin Harrison, 1833–1901; Chronology, Documents, Bibliographical Aids*. Dobbs Ferry, NY: Oceana Publications, 1969.

———. *Benjamin Harrison: Hoosier Warrior (Through the Civil War Years, 1833–1865)*. New York: University Publishers, 1952.

———. *Benjamin Harrison: Hoosier Statesman (From the Civil War to the White House, 1865–1888)*. New York: University Publishers, 1959.

———. *Benjamin Harrison: Hoosier President (The White House and After)*. Indianapolis: Bobbs-Merrill Company, 1968.

Socolofsky, Homer E., and Allan B. Spetter. *The Presidency of Benjamin Harrison*. Lawrence: University Press of Kansas, 1987.

Talley, Steve. *Bland Ambition: From Adams to Quayle—The Cranks, Criminals, Tax Cheats, and Golfers Who Made It to Vice President*. San Diego: Harcourt Brace Jovanovich, 1992.

Thornbrough, Emma Lou. *Indiana in the Civil War Era, 1850–1880*. 1965. Reprint, Indianapolis: Indiana Historical Society, 1989.

Troy, Gil. *See How They Ran: The Changing Role of the Presidential Candidate*. 1991; Revised and Expanded Edition. Cambridge: Harvard University Press, 1996.

Upchurch, Thomas Adams. *Legislating Racism: The Billion Dollar Congress and the Birth of Jim Crow*. Lexington: University Press of Kentucky, 2004.

Volwiler, Albert T. *The Correspondence between Benjamin Harrison and James G. Blaine, 1882–1893*. Philadelphia, PA: American Philosophical Society, 1940.

Wallace, Lew. *Life of Gen. Ben Harrison*. 1888. Reprint. Crawfordsville, IN: Lew Wallace Study Preservation Society, 2017.

Watson, Robert P. *First Ladies of the United States: A Biographical Dictionary*. Boulder, CO: Lynne Rienner Publishers, 2001.

White, Richard. *The Republic for Which It Stands: The United States during Reconstruction and the Gilded Age, 1865–1896*. New York: Oxford University Press, 2017.

White, William Allen. *Masks in a Pageant*. 1928. Reprint. Westport, CT: Greenwood Press, 1971.

Index